# Psyche's Stories

# Psyche's Stories

## Modern Jungian Interpretations of Fairy Tales

EDITED BY MURRAY STEIN AND LIONEL CORBETT

### Volume Three

CHIRON PUBLICATIONS
WILMETTE, ILLINOIS

Library of Congress Catalog Card Number: 90-26108

Printed in the United States of America.
Copyediting by Susan C. Roberts.
Book design by Siobhan Drummond.
Original art by April Uhlir.

**Library of Congress Cataloging-in-Publication Data:**

(Revised for vol. 3)

Psyche's Stories

   Includes bibliographical references.
   1. Jung, C. G. (Carl Gustav), 1875–1961.
2. Fairy tales – History and criticism.
3. Psychoanalysis and folklore. 4. Archetype
(Psychology). I. Stein, Murray, 1943–
II. Corbett, Lionel.
GR550P78    1991       398'.019    90-26108

ISBN 978-0-933029-90-3

# Contents

# "The White Snake"
# A Psychological Hero's Journey

## Murray Stein

When entertainment moved off the stages of vaudeville to radio, one of the old professional comedians observed how much material this new medium consumed. On the vaudeville circuit he could use the same jokes over and over again because the audiences were always different, but on radio he played again and again to the same audience and so could not repeat his lines. The laugh meter dropped sharply even for jokes used only once before. His clever stories were instantly used up.

Great stories, on the other hand, are never consumed. They are like the porridge pot that cannot be emptied: no matter how often you go back, you always find more food. You can read or hear great stories many times, but each repeat brings a new insight or a fresh realization. Great stories yield not only enjoyment but a fresh experience each time they are read or heard; they are a rich meal for digestion.

This became especially vivid for me several years ago when a friend made what seemed an extraordinary comment. Why, she wondered, do people keep going back to church year after year once they've heard the whole story and been through the cycle of Christmas, Lent, Easter, Pentecost, and so on a few times? "Once you've got it, why keep on doing it?" she asked in slightly mock wonder.

As though participating in religious ritual were like going to the movies! Thus, if we don't usually see the same movie over and over, why repeat religious ritual so often? Is it a compulsion? Being a psychologist, moreover, my friend thought quite naturally in pathological terms, and this looked to her like a repetition compulsion. (Freud suggested the same interpretation in *Totem and Taboo*.)

Religious rituals are inexhaustible, however, and the reason for repeating them is that they keep yielding new depth and meaning. Nor are the truly great stories ever depleted of meaning. There is always more to reflect on, more nourishment to draw out of them. As great stories are reexperienced, new thoughts make their way into consciousness and our mental horizons expand with surprisingly fresh content.

Myths are such stories, and within the setting of living religions they function as defining statements. They express in image and narrative form what the religion is essentially all about.

I realized this one Easter morning. Easter Sunday celebrates the risen Christ. On this particular occasion, trumpets were brought out in the church, the organist pulled out all the stops, and the hymns and sermon retold the story of Jesus' miraculous victory over darkness and death. And then there occurred an abrupt shift in mood and tone: the celebration's jubilant spirit subsided and the somber tones of the Eucharistic prayer began. The story line backed up to the days before Easter. We were in the upper room again, the bread was being broken and the wine blessed, and "the body that was broken for you" became the central image for reflection. Why this retreat from the glory of Easter? Why this repetition of what was supposed to belong decisively to the past? Why back up now to remember yet again how the Lord died when we were supposed to be celebrating the fact that he lived?

The story seemed to have lost its forward momentum, and we were pulled back to sacrifice, to the cross, and to expiatory death. But this is the defining moment for Christianity, I realized. Its essence is captured by what happened on the night in which Jesus was betrayed and shortly thereafter hung on the tree. "Don't forget it!" is the message. That is the deepest well out of which Christianity has pulled its meaning and identity. As the experience of the Passover defines Judaism, the Last

Supper and the cross define Christianity. They are the "big bang" moments that create religious traditions that extend over millennia.

Great stories become defining moments in the lives of individuals, too. These are the experiences, told and retold many times over the course of years, which sum up the essence of a person's life. In the course of a full Jungian analysis, many dreams will be reported, discussed, and digested, but one or two will stand out as the defining stories of this psyche. These state in a highly condensed form what this personality is all about or what the direction of the analysis has been or will become. They are symbols, and they become the source for guidance, the well out of which inspiration and refreshment are drawn many times, perhaps for all of life.

Other sorts of stories also play a role in defining central features of an individual. Hans Dieckman, a German Jungian analyst, wrote a classic paper on the subject of the favorite fairy tale from childhood (now available as a chapter in his book, *Twice-Told Tales*). He discovered that a person's favorite fairy tale from childhood contained themes and issues that turned out to be central to analysis later in adulthood. Again, these are stories that contain essential human themes and have perennial meaning and value. What the psyche selects and retains and replays repeatedly is highly significant. The psyche may be pluralistic at one level (cf. Samuels 1989), but at other, and I believe deeper and more important, levels the individual psyche is structured by a few basic patterns that manifest in many ways and at many different times throughout a person's lifetime.

The fairy tale I am investigating here has stayed with me for over twenty years. Originally I chose it as the subject for an academic exercise, to fulfill an assignment at the Jung Institute in Zurich to interpret a fairy tale. "The White Snake" caught my eye at first because of its unusual title. I had never read it or heard it before, and this by itself intrigued me. The interpretation I wrote then is, in retrospect, a bit stilted and patched together with theory. Having lived with the story for quite a long time now, I find that its meaning and relevance have increased for me. Today, this tale strikes me as one of those great stories that is utterly inexhaustible. Each reading is a fresh experience, and the possibilities it offers for reflection seem almost endless.

## *The White Snake*

A long time ago there lived a king who was famous for his wisdom. In his kingdom were no secrets that he did not know about. It was his practice every day after dinner to ask his trusted servant to bring him a covered dish. The servant then had to leave the room. No one knew what was on the dish, for the king never lifted the cover until he was alone.

One day as the servant carries the dish out of the room he is overcome with curiosity. He takes it to his own room, closes the door, and lifts the cover. There on the platter he sees a white snake. Having gone this far, he thinks he will also try tasting it, so he cuts off a bit of the snake and eats it. Suddenly he hears voices chattering outside his window. It is the sparrows, and they are talking about what they have seen around the kingdom that morning. The servant has received the ability to understand the language of animals.

On the very day this happens the queen loses her most precious ring, and suspicion falls on the trusted servant because he is allowed to go everywhere in the palace. The king confronts him and threatens that if he does not produce the thief by tomorrow he will be executed. Naturally the servant protests his innocence, but it is of no use.

It is with a heavy heart that he goes out into the courtyard, wondering how he will defend himself against this false accusation. Outside he overhears some ducks having a quiet conversation as they smooth their feathers and take a rest beside the brook. They are discussing their breakfast, and one of them says: "Something is bothering my stomach; I was eating too fast and I swallowed a ring that was lying under the queen's window." The servant realizes this is the thief, so he grabs the duck and takes her to the cook, who, seeing what a nice fat bird she is, cuts off her head and prepares her for dinner. As he does so, he finds the queen's ring and the servant is exonerated.

The king is sorry for his error and wants to make up for jumping to a false conclusion, so he offers the servant his choice of positions at court. But the servant turns down the offer and asks only for a horse and a little money. He wants to explore the world on his own a little. The king grants his request, and the servant sets out.

After a time he comes to a pond where he sees three fishes caught in reeds and dying for lack of water. Our hero on horseback hears them complaining about their bad luck and has pity on them, freeing them and returning them to the pond. As he goes on his way, they cry out to him: "We will remember you and repay you for saving us."

He rides on, and soon he overhears some tiny voices in the sand under his horse's hooves. He stops to listen and hears an ant king complaining about the insensitive horse that is treading on his people without mercy. So the hero turns his horse off onto a side path, and as he passes the ant king cries out to him: "We will remember you – one good turn deserves another!"

As he continues on his way, he comes upon two old ravens throwing their young out of their nest and screaming at them to learn to take care of themselves. But the little ravens are still young and helpless, and they fall to the ground where they cry out and complain that they will starve to death. So the good man, filled with compassion for the abandoned young ravens, dismounts, kills his horse with his sword, and lets the little birds feed on its carcass. With gratitude they cry out: "We will remember you – one good turn deserves another!"

Now the hero must go ahead on his own two legs. After a time he enters a large city and hears an announcement in the streets that the king's daughter is looking for a husband. Whoever would seek her hand must complete a hard task, however, and if he fails he will forfeit his life. The young man hears that many have already failed. Nevertheless, when he sees the princess he is smitten by her beauty, and, despite the grave risk, he presents himself as a suitor.

The hard task follows. The king takes him down to the sea and tosses a gold ring into the waves. The task is to bring the ring back up out of the choppy waters; what is more, he will be thrown back into sea until he either comes up with the ring or drowns. As the young man stands on the shore wondering what will become of him now, some fish suddenly surface whom he recognizes as the ones he had saved. One of them places a mussel at his feet, and when he opens it he finds the ring. With great joy he takes the ring to the king and asks for his reward.

The princess is proud, however, and does not want to accept so humble a suitor, so she proposes a second hard task. This time she leads the way. In the garden, she opens ten sacks filled with millet seed which she scatters in the grass with her own hands. If the suitor has not returned every grain of millet to the sacks by morning, he will be executed. Again the young man feels helpless and wonders what will become of him. He sits in the garden through the night, and as dawn lights the sky he realizes that the sacks are full and not a single grain of millet has been left on the ground. The ant king has come in the night with his subjects, and they have repaid his earlier kindness.

Yet when the princess comes out in the morning and sees that the task has been completed, her proud heart still resists. And so she proposes a third hard task: if he wants to become her husband, the young man must bring her an apple from the Tree of Life. The suitor does not know where the Tree of Life is to be found, but he sets out anyway and walks for as long as his legs will carry him. He wanders through three kingdoms, and one evening he comes to a wood and lies down under a tree to sleep. In the branches above him he suddenly hears some rustling, and a golden apple falls into his hand. Three ravens follow it, fly down and perch on his knee. They tell him that they are the ones he saved by killing his horse, and that when they heard about his quest for an apple from the Tree of Life they flew over the sea to the end of the world, where the Tree stands, and brought one back for him.

The suitor carries the golden apple back to the princess, who now has no more cause to resist him. They cut the Apple of Life in two and eat it together. Then her heart opens, and she becomes filled with love for him, and they live in happiness to a great age.

## PART I: THE WAY OF THE SERPENT

Even on a first reading, this is a good story. It is beautifully balanced, and the moments of dramatic tension build and resolve in a satisfying way. To my knowledge, no movie or opera has been based on this script, but Mozart could certainly have composed a wonderful, magical rendition of it had he set his mind to it.

This is the story of a man who undergoes initiation and rises to fame and fortune by virtue of his sweet character, courage, and faith. In one sense, it is a story of the Horatio Alger type, a from-servant-to-king story. But what makes it a truly great and fascinating story arises from the symbolical level. A glimpse into what is going on symbolically in this story opens up an immense horizon of meaning. This is one of those stories you can return to again and again and never exhaust it, a story that you can think about for a long, long time.

What makes it so special and suggestive lies in the imagery. There are resonances with the Bible, with Greek myth, with reli-

gious ritual, with alchemy. These associations create reverbera-
tions throughout the universe of symbols and set up a thunder-
ous symphony of thoughts. The hard task in what follows is to
tune into it, even if we cannot possibly capture the whole.

In the first movement of this symphony, to stay with the
metaphor, the main theme involves the image of the white snake
and the idea of understanding the language of animals. The story
opens with an implied statement that once, long ago, there was a
wise king who knew everything that went on in his land because
every day he ate a piece of a white snake. This gave him the
ability to understand the language of animals, and by listening to
them he was informed of everything that was going on. There are
no secrets in his kingdom. This is a king with full consciousness
of everything that is going on in the whole land.

As a psychological statement, this image tells us that there is
no repression in this psychic system, no defensive network or set
of complexes blocking communication between the upper reaches
of conscious life and the depths of somatic existence. This is an
extraordinarily healthy state. It is, in fact, the definition of psychological wholeness.

One notable feature of this situation is the suggestion that
the king's omniscience depends upon his daily contact with the
white snake. This king is not like the biblical God, whose omniscience is understood to depend on nothing outside of himself.
The God of the biblical tradition does not need to consult anyone
or be in contact with anything outside of himself in order to
maintain complete conscious knowledge of what is going on in his
kingdom (except in the Book of Job, where Yahweh consults with
Satan, who goes up and down in the world and reports back to
him about goings-on there). Yahweh is not dependent on the
white snake for his wisdom. So the king is not God, and his
wisdom is contingent. The white snake is the source.

Yahweh and the king of our story do, however, show a similar
tendency to lapse from their omniscience, somehow forgetting to
consult it at crucial moments. Yahweh does this when he
instructs Adam to avoid eating from the tree of knowledge of
good and evil (Gen. 2:16–17) but does not look ahead far enough
to know that this admonition will not keep him from doing precisely the forbidden thing. The fairy-tale king in our story has a
puzzling lapse when he falsely accuses his trusted servant of
stealing the queen's ring when he could as easily have listened to
the animals for a few moments and picked up the correct answer.

As it turns out, in both stories the lapse in omniscience is strangely necessary. Without it there would be no story, only an endless state of peace and harmony; time would stand still, nothing would happen, paradise would prevail. It seems that some amount of failure is necessary in order for development to take place.

Back to the snake. The king's omniscience depends on a daily meal of white snake. The daily ritual of eating a symbolic meal is a familiar one in Western religion, for every day the Holy Eucharist is served in Catholic churches, and every day the priesthood has traditionally partaken of the sanctified bread and wine. The spiritual nature of this meal is clearly symbolized in the fairy tale by the snake's whiteness. This is a highly unusual and unnatural color for a snake. White is the color of light, purity, perfection. It is usually associated with the absolute and consequently is often used in marriage rituals, initiations, and death rites. Priests often wear white garments to symbolize spirit and light, and angels are clothed in white for the same reason. It is clear, therefore, that the king's wisdom depends upon a ritual of daily nourishment with spiritual food.

That this spiritual food is represented by a serpent, however, marks a sharp departure from Christianity. This king is not a good Catholic who goes to Mass every day. The serpent, in the biblical tradition, is representative of evil, not of good. This may be due to the ancient association of the serpent (along with the pig) with the Great Mother and her religions in the Near East. As the patriarchal Yahweh religion established itself, it excoriated the sacred symbols of the neighboring religions. Yahweh put enmity between Eve and the serpent, and this also signified the hostility between Yahwistic religion and the serpent worshipers (cf. Meador 1992, pp. 118ff). If we follow Erich Neumann's line of thought in *The Great Mother* and *The Origins and History of Consciousness* and Phyllis Moore's argument in *No Other Gods*, Yahwistic religion created a new kind of "mental ego," which we recognize today as an intact center of consciousness located in the head and having minimal contact with and awareness of the instincts and the body. What was gained by this development was a strong sense of linear time, an increased emphasis on mind over matter, and more ego autonomy. This was necessary in order to go out and conquer the world, manage it, and build the sort of mental disciplines that eventually made modern scientific and technological achievements possible. This has been the gift of the biblical development, and it has provided the dynamic element in Western societies. All of this has been done without the help of serpent wisdom.

What was lost when the connection with the serpent was severed? This is a question that has only been asked in recent times and is still far from being fully answered. It has to do with the connection to the unconscious and knowledge of the spirit in the body, in nature, and in matter. By severing consciousness of the serpent, a head-centered type of ego was created that repressed its connection to the body, to nature, to the animal instincts within and to the animals in the world without. All of these became the "unconscious."

If we compare the biblical religions to Native American religions, for example, we can see a stark difference in sensibility. Where the Native Americans would pray to animals, the biblical religionists were instructed to dominate them – hence our modern agribusiness, our grotesque animal farms, and our sterile supermarkets. Connection to the earth, to the spirits residing in the natural world, to the inner life of things, is strong and nourished in the one and utterly absent (theologically) from the other. The difference between Western and Oriental medicine points up a similar divergence in attitude toward nature and especially toward the body: the one cuts, treats, and hospitalizes and the other consults, listens to, and tends the body.

The same difference can be seen in attitudes taken toward the unconscious by the pragmatic, rational ego psychologies and by Jungian psychology. The former condition, train, desensitize, and manipulate the unconscious for the ego's ends and purposes; the latter attends to, listens to, and tries to understand the unconscious as it shows itself in dreams, fantasies, and synchronicities. More than its theories, it is this attitude of listening for the voice of the spirit hidden away in the body, in the instincts, and in nature that characterizes Jungian psychology and analysis. This is also what the fairy-tale king, and later the trusted servant, do. Not only do they listen to the voices of the animals, but they can understand what the animals are saying in their own languages.

The white snake is Mercurius, spirit of the unconscious (cf. Jung 1948). Ambisexual – male and female – sometimes one and sometimes the other, he and/or she is the king-queen of the unconscious and the spirit in nature. Jung speaks of Mercurius, whom the alchemists regarded as central in their work, as the son of the

Mother and as one who states the answer from the collective unconscious to the dogmatic image of Christ, the son of the Father and the psychological dominant of collective consciousness. Mercurius represents the spiritual life within the darkness of matter, the soul in the world around us, a spirit who, unlike our theological God, is not cut off and separate or located in a removed and transcendent place but is found everywhere and yet is extremely hard to pin down.

The fairy tale speaks of an original situation (*in illo tempore*, as Eliade would call it), in which the central principle of consciousness, the king, was in touch with the spirit of nature. This antedates Yahweh, and in personalistic psychological development it precedes the oedipal stage. It speaks of a state that we could call original wholeness. In that time, as infants, we were in communication with the whole, and we could understand the language of nature. This is a state of preconscious wholeness, "conscious" being defined as postrepression existence.

But then we lost it, collectively and individually. If we were educated within the patriarchal medium, in which the biblical religions form the center of value and spiritual awareness, we lost contact with the spirit Mercurius. Today we stand in awe of those who have not lost it, who are still in touch with original wholeness and who understand the language of the unconscious, of the body, of nature. Such persons are utterly foreign to us, and we watch in wonder and amazement at what they can do and at what they know. They are magical. Of course, we may think they are simply unaware of how much they are projecting into the world, and in that case we can make the judgment that they are merely preconscious. Luckily, anthropologists have taught us to be careful about our Western cultural assumptions when observing non-Western peoples. The epistemological problem is not as simple as it may appear at first glance: Who is projecting, the observer or the observed?

When the servant breaks the rule and looks into the dish and eats a piece of the snake, he magically regains this original connection with the spirit of the unconscious. He, too, can now listen to the animals and understand what they are saying. But for us, it is not usually so easy to regain this ability. It is not a matter of an instant transformation through one quick initiation. Most of us have to work through the thick walls of complexes that stand between us and the spirit Mercurius. We have to learn the language of the unconscious in a painstaking way, like an adult trying to learn a foreign language. The body tightens up, and we don't understand the message. An accident occurs, and we have an inkling that it means something, that a complex is active, but we cannot understand clearly. What is going on here? we wonder. Someone tells us a dream, and we have no idea what it is saying. What is this strange hieroglyphical language of image and symbol? We don't believe that the animals really have a language, that they have feelings, that they want to communicate something or have anything to say. Do we recognize the wisdom of the owl, the wiliness of the coyote, the regal nature of the lion? We go to the zoo and look at these animals behind bars and what do we see? Emptiness. If there is a message here and nature has something to say, what is it?

But imagine that you have been initiated; you have been granted the ability to understand the language of animals and the privilege of coming into contact daily with the spirit of the unconscious, Mercurius. You would wake up in the morning and know the meaning of your dreams. Your dreams would tell you what is going on in the kingdom of the psyche within and without. Your dreams know many things that your conscious ego has no inkling of, things from far away, things about other people, things about nature and spiritual realms beyond the five senses. Dreams could teach you about the spirits; about good and evil; about the psychological condition of family members; about the state of affairs in the political world; about the cosmos. There is almost no limit to what you could learn if you could understand the language of your dreams.

If you walked outdoors, you could receive news from the birds, from the squirrels, from the geese and ducks returning from their winter in the south. The trees and bushes, the grass, even the stones would tell you things about their condition. Your consciousness would be filled with information and news from the four corners of the world.

As far-fetched as this sounds, it is the condition of the sage. The sage is someone who can listen to tones and sounds beyond the range of others, who can read the body language of strangers and understand what they are saying behind their masks of words, who can understand a dream without looking up the symbols in a dictionary. Our fairy tale tells us that acquiring this ability is as easy as eating a piece of the white snake. But we also know that finding the white snake is as tricky as finding the Grail castle. Mercurius is slippery, and if you think you have him in your fist, he is sure to escape and leave you empty-handed. And yet Mercurius is everywhere and is our natural birthright. We all "have" an unconscious, we all have dreams, and we all have access to the spirit of wholeness. Why is something so easy also so hard? This must be the question of every person who has ever seriously entered upon a spiritual path, or undertaken the work of individuation. Finding Mercurius and eating of him seems to be the key.

## PART II: THE SACRIFICE

While it is obviously true that most jokes wear out if you tell them repeatedly to the same audience, it also seems that great stories never lose their appeal because they always suggest something more to think about. The great stories continue to affect us deeply, both emotionally and intellectually, because they contain symbols. In fact, the stories, or central parts of them, are themselves symbols. Symbols connect us to mystery and to the very farthest horizons of conceivable meaning.

Thus far I have been looking at "The White Snake" from a symbolic viewpoint that lifts its meaning beyond the concrete details and gives us something to think about. To treat the white snake as a "symbol," however, does not require overlooking its sexual and phallic associations. A straightforward oedipal interpretation of this story is not only possible but cogent and can add to its meaning as long as these insights remain symbolic.

When the servant eats of the king's white snake, he breaks a taboo. He is initiated into the phallic mysteries of the king's wisdom. But this is an oedipal violation, which interferes not only with the king's wisdom but, oddly, with his relationship to the queen. She loses her most precious ring, a symbol of her relationship to the king. All of this is quite unconscious and produces only an indirect symptom: the servant is accused of causing the problem and is threatened with punishment.

In order to avoid this punishment, the servant has to restore the royal couple's relationship and leave the kingdom. This he does. And eventually he finds his own sexual partner, the princess, and through hard tasks and suffering is able to get her to open up to him. In other words, he finally wins the goal that was set before him by his initiation into phallic sexuality when he ate the white snake.

If this were all the story was about—an oedipal triumph—we would have little more to think about. By this method, however, the symbols in the story are not dealt with but avoided or reduced to concrete hidden meanings. What does it mean that the snake is white and not black or green? Why is there a golden apple from the Tree of Life at the end of the story? Such images beg for more and keep us from stopping with a concrete oedipal interpretation.

And yet the oedipal interpretation is important to keep in mind because it is definitely a theme in the story. The question is, what does this theme mean, particularly in the context of the other images and associations in the tale? The phallic mystery is central, but as a mystery, it connects us to more than the issue of sexual development.

In speaking about symbols as connecting links, I am falling back on the ancient understanding of the word *symbol*. Etymologically, it is derived from the Greek *symbolon*, the word for a coin that had been broken in two. Two business partners would each get one of these pieces and would unite the pieces to indicate the inception of partnership. The restored coin was the *symbolon*, representing the connection between the two parties.

When we use the word *symbol* in a psychological sense, i.e., intrapsychically, what we have in mind is images, words, concepts, sounds, or whatever does the job of connecting the conscious part of the psyche (centered by the ego) with another part (a complex, an instinct, an archetype). And because the part to which the symbol connects the ego is unconscious, there is an aura of fascination around the symbol. The symbol glows with mystery. We say it is "numinous." And the more strongly it glows, the more numinous it is, the closer it comes to connecting the ego to the Self.

In "The White Snake," a transformation occurs when the servant eats a piece of the snake and suddenly is able to understand the language of animals. At this moment, he receives what the king has: a kind of knowledge that will forever change his consciousness. He receives the mystery and is now an initiate. This transformation of his consciousness through the eating of the white snake opens the channel to the unconscious, making its contents available to him. So in this way the white snake itself functions as a symbol in the story: it connects ego-consciousness, as represented by the servant, to another realm, the intelligent animal realm.

In one sense, the snake in our story may represent a compensation, a polarity, to the Christian symbol of the Mass. While the symbol of the Mass connects ego-consciousness to the spiritual realm, the symbol of the white snake connects it to the animal realm. In another respect, however, they are not so different: the white snake actually connects ego-consciousness to the *spirit* in the animal realm, to the language of the animals, i.e., to their consciousness, and thus to the deeper level of spirit in matter. In this respect, this fairy tale is in agreement with the purpose of the alchemical opus, which was to find, work with, and finally save the spirit locked away or hidden in matter. This spirit in matter was conceived to be the same as the divine spirit, only in a "fallen" form. After all, spirit is spirit, wherever you find it. (I will pursue this alchemical parallel more fully later.) Thus both the white snake and the Mass function to connect the ego to spirit (Mercurius and Christ, respectively).

Once our hero has touched the symbolic object and has taken in the symbolic food, his ears are opened, and he is made aware of a dimension of existence hitherto inaccessible to him. He becomes aware of the unconscious and its intelligence and spirit. Insofar as this is similar to a conversion experience, where a person is suddenly opened to the spiritual dimension of life, this represents the servant's conversion. And the next thing that happens is that the king falsely accuses him of stealing. This cannot be an accident, and it sets in motion the chain of events that leads him to a fateful choice. He is offered the highest seat in the realm besides that of the king, a sort of oedipal triumph or at least exoneration. But instead of accepting the offer, he asks to be released from service and given a horse and some money. He wants to see the world a little. And so it comes about that he separates himself from the realm of the king he has served faithfully until now.

This chain of events, from the conversion of consciousness via the experience of the symbol to the volitional separation from servitude and the embrace of personal freedom, bears further reflection.

Asking to be freed from the king's service is our hero's second major decision in the story. (The first was to uncover the dish and taste the white snake.) Now he relinquishes the honor of being closely associated with the king and chooses autonomy instead. This second choice is consistent with the first: in both he shows a strong tendency toward independence. The second choice carries him further in this direction than the first, although without the transformation effected by the experience of the white snake, the choice of this much independence might not have been so significant. In a sense he was free of the king's authority all along, since he was able to make the choice to break the taboo and look under the cover. But now he takes a decisive step, explicitly freeing himself not only from the king's service but his protection. In developmental terms, he is choosing to leave the stage of dependency on omnipotent/omniscient parents – the king and queen – and to venture forth into life on his own. The king has unwittingly helped him do this by falsely accusing him of a crime and threatening to end his life. When the king broke faith, he unconsciously served notice to the servant that it was no longer safe to remain in the kingdom. This breech of trust made it easier for the servant to shed his bondage to the king, and yet the choice still required the sacrifice of the opportunity to sit at the king's right hand.

This sacrifice is all the more notable in view of the end of the story, where the servant rises to the position of inheriting a kingdom for himself. At the earlier moment, he walks away from what would have amounted to an oedipal struggle for someone else's kingdom in order to go out and win his own. But he can do this only because he has experienced the phallic mystery of the white snake for himself. This experience has given him the essence of the king's wisdom by opening up access to the same source of knowledge that has been available to the wise king. Once this transformation of consciousness has been accomplished, the servant can venture out and succeed in finding his own fortune. The fact that, by breaking trust, the king unwittingly helps him leave is but one more piece in the dynamic that is driving the hero's own individuation process toward its triumphant conclusion at the end of the story.

Leaving the kingdom of the wise king is a significant step on the way to the hero's own individuation, for it represents his independence from heteronomous authority and the power of the past and signifies his openness and freedom to pursue a new future. It is equivalent to leaving childhood behind, although in this case without losing the magical connection to the archetypal world that is the native gift of childhood.

A man or woman makes this same sacrifice of dependency when he or she leaves a large organization – a corporation, a university, a governmental agency – in which protection and benefits abound and fame and power seem within reach, but at the price of freedom and creativity. The person ventures out beyond the parental guardians and powers into the great unknown to see the world a little. If we wonder why some can take such risks and others cannot, it may be instructive to think of our fairy tale and realize that it may depend upon whether one has eaten of the white snake. The self-assurance provided by this connection to the unconscious is crucial. It means that the parental complexes, father and mother, are not in control of the ego any longer.

The gift of understanding the language of animals does not fail our hero as he sets out on his horse, for soon he comes upon three fish that have gotten tangled in some reeds and are complaining about their bad luck. He hears their conversation, he understands it, and more than that, he acts on what he hears and understands, freeing the fish and returning them to the water. This act of compassion will be repeated three times, with each instance being a little more remarkable than the last. The first is a more or less casual act of empathy and indicates that the hero has a good heart. The second – when he overhears the ant king complaining about the trampling of his tiny subjects and directs his horse to take another path – is more surprising because of the degree of attunement it reveals: from horseback, who could possibly hear an ant's voice? But of all the hero's acts of compassion, the third is surely the most astonishing. He overhears a pair of old ravens complaining about their young and sees them throw their fledglings out of the nest. He hears the young birds crying, "Oh, what helpless chicks we are! We must shift for ourselves, and yet we cannot fly! What can we do but lie here and starve?" So (to this reader's everlasting astonishment) he gets down from his horse, pulls his sword from its sheath, and kills his horse. He feeds the raven chicks his one and only horse. And this brings us to the unavoidable conclusion that sacrifice is the second great symbol in this story.

The hero's sensitivity and empathy for the animals he confronts on his journey are truly extraordinary. What a heart he has! Does this empathy also derive from his numinous experience, the eating of the white snake? The story does not tell us, and the most we can say is that this hero shows uncommon qualities in this respect. His courage and independence are admirable but to be expected; his sensitivity to animals in trouble, to the troubled spirit of the animals he finds on his journey, is remarkable and surprising. But most astonishing of all is his act of sacrificing his horse for the young ravens.

Jung makes an interesting and important distinction between a gift and a sacrifice:

When . . . I give away something that is "mine," what I am giving is essentially a symbol, a thing of many meanings; but, owing to my unconsciousness of its symbolic character, it adheres to my ego, because it is part of my personality. Hence there is always an unspoken "give that thou mayest receive." Consequently the gift always carries with it an intention, for the mere giving of it is not a sacrifice. It only becomes a sacrifice if I give up the implied intention of receiving something in return. If it is to be a true sacrifice, the gift must be given as if it were being destroyed. Only then is it possible for the egoist claim to be given up.

What I sacrifice is my own selfish claim, and by doing this I give up myself. Every sacrifice is therefore, to a greater or lesser degree, a self-sacrifice. The degree to which it is so depends on the significance of the gift. If it is of great value to me and touches my most personal feelings, I can be sure that in giving up my egoistic claim I shall challenge my ego personality to revolt. I can also be sure that the power which suppresses this claim, and thus suppresses me, must be the self. Hence it is the self that causes me to make the sacrifice; nay more, it compels me to make it. The self is the sacrificer, and I am the sacrificed gift, the human sacrifice. (Jung 1954a, pars. 390, 397)

The idea is that if it is a mere "gift," the ego's attachment and identification with it remains and strings are attached. But if a sacrifice is made, the identification with the object is relinquished and the ego's claims are overridden in favor of the claims of the Self. I think this applies to the hero's killing of his horse for the young ravens in our tale. The horse, to which the young man is attached, represents a part of himself; it is his possession, his inheritance from the wise king whom he faithfully served. Were he "giving" the horse away, making a gift of him, he would expect a payment of equal value in return. By slaying the horse and using it to feed the young ravens without thought of return on an "investment," he relinquishes his ego claim. The story is saying he makes a sacrifice here, a horse sacrifice. There is no rational calculation in this, either; after all, are ravens worth more than a horse? And if you asked the hero why he did this, he would have to say, with Jung, "The Self made me do it!" It is a nonrational, extreme action, and he does it without consulting the horse's feelings either!

With each act of compassion our young hero sacrifices some bit of his ego. Stopping to help the fish, he delays his journey forward a little; he slows down. In so doing he makes a relation-

ship with the fish, who will eventually return his gesture of empathy by bringing the ring up out of the sea. In making this connection to the fish, the hero establishes a relationship with his own
unconscious that goes beyond merely understanding its language. This is an active, caring relationship that produces reciprocity, and this reciprocity between conscious and unconscious
forms a dynamic that is essential for creative living. The fish
represent autonomous contents of the psychic depths, such as the
instincts (fish are often associated with sexuality, hence their
connection to the ring later in the story). They can offer creative
resources to the ego if a positive relationship exists.

If the first sacrifice established the hero's positive relationship to the depths of his instinctive unconscious, the second
sacrifice – bypassing the kingdom of the ant king – represents his
empathic sensitivity to the tiniest nuances of physical and communal existence. Both the physical world and the social world
depend on precise organization and the diligent, day in, day out
workings of millions of coordinated energy units. Through his
sacrificial gesture – going out of his way to avoid trampling on
the sensitive network on the ground – our hero forms a positive
relationship with this level of life. This relationship will come to
his assistance later when his own life will depend on this kind of
organized effort. Attention to the everyday needs of our bodies,
our society, and our natural environment costs us some of our
ego's drive for pursuing its own direction. Ants are also associated with fertility, as is millet; hence we can say that organized
fertility (families, agriculture, etc.) forms the basis for sustaining
life in its physical and social manifestations.

The sacrificial acts culminate in the hero slaying his horse for
the young ravens. This act seems disproportionate – a horse for a
few little ravens – until we realize its symbolic meaning. For the
hero, sacrificing his horse meant letting go of the ego claims still
attached to his parental household, to the kingdom from which he
came and from which he inherited the horse. It is as though he
gave away his inheritance to an orphanage. Now he has to proceed on his own two legs. So this remarkable act of sacrifice also
frees him from the last shred of dependence on and attachment to
his past. He has finally put the past behind him completely. But
the horse also represents the hero's somatic unconscious – the
unconsciousness housed in his body and in his physical
instincts – and by sacrificing this for the ravens, he greatly adds

to the symbolic value, to the energic gradient, of the psychic factor represented by the raven.

As birds, ravens symbolize the spiritual end of the psychic spectrum (cf. Jung 1954b, pars. 379ff) and thus stand in contrast to the fish and especially to the ants. In his first two acts of empathy, the hero formed a positive relationship to the instinctual unconscious and to the collective working organization on which life depends; in his third act, the major sacrifice, he creates a bond to the spiritual dimension. And in the end, it is the ravens who deliver the golden apple from the Tree of Life.

In this middle section of our fairy tale, then, we see the hero establishing the psychological basis for his individuation process. Through sacrifice, the ego creates a positive relationship with the other, unconscious parts of the psyche. We see that now the ego has managed to ally itself with both ends of the psychic spectrum, the instinctual and spiritual, matter and spirit. And because the ego has done this work, it can move forward with the confidence that it will be supported from within and without in times of need and crisis.

It seems to me that this middle section of the story outlines in barest symbolic form the essential steps that all of us must take in order to individuate personally and meet the grave collective crises of our time. First, we must learn the language of the animals, that is, we must learn how to understand the cries for help coming from all that is around us: from the unconscious in the form of dreams; from the body in symptoms and reactions to the surrounding world; from society in its collective and political illnesses; from our earth in its environmental crises; and from our own poverty-stricken and orphaned spirits in the form of depressions, addictions, or acts of desperation. Understanding these cries for help is the first step. It entails eating of the white snake – gaining knowledge of the unconscious psyche and learning to think and feel symbolically, with psychic sensitivity to the world within and without.

Beyond that – and that is a tall enough order in itself – we must also act on what we hear and understand. Simply understanding the language of the suffering animals will not further our individuation. This is what Jung sometimes referred to as the aesthetic stage of interpretation: we remember the dream, we interpret it, we make it vivid through painting or dance or drawing. But we have not yet acted on it. That requires what he called the ethical step, or doing something with what we know. This is where the theme of sacrifice enters. For the ego to act on what it knows and understands inevitably entails a sacrifice of ego. As with the young hero of the tale, it means taking time, altering one's plans, and spending one's inheritance on a spiritual investment. We must take care of the trees and animals and return them to their natural environment. We must stop paving over the ant kingdoms with asphalt and concrete and turning farmland into parking lots, shopping malls, and highways. We must take care of our communal life in cities, towns, and rural areas. We must develop much greater sensitivity to what our bodies want and need instead of investing more in gross allopathic treatment plants, i.e., modern hospitals. And finally, and perhaps most important of all, we must forfeit our egos for the sake of new spiritual possibilities. We are rich in things and extremely poor in spirit. If we cling to our horses – our big cars, our wasteful lifestyles, our selfish interests – we will never find the golden apple because such "horses" cannot carry us to the Tree of Life. And we ourselves don't even know where such a tree is or how to go about finding it. Only the ravens, these dark thoughts of the spirit that the alchemists associated with the *nigredo* stage of the opus, can traverse the distance and bring back the gold. So the first step is to recognize our need – our lack of spiritual resources, our inability to feed ourselves spiritually, our abandonment by and disconnection from our parental spiritual traditions – and then sacrifice our ego's drives so we may begin to hear the still, small voices within this spiritual want. What is more, ours must be a spontaneous, openhearted, and affirmative sacrifice with nothing asked in return. Take, eat, this is my body broken for you. We have the example.

To conclude this portion of our reflections, I would like to raise one more point about genuine symbols. Most of us have had some experience of a "living symbol." It may be an image, a ritual, an idea, or a dream. It may have been experienced in a collective setting – a religious ceremony, for instance – or in private, as with a dream or a personal ritual. Such a symbol, when it lives for us, has the property of endurance through time. We can go back to it in memory or we can repeat it. In so doing, we reconstitute the experience in some way and contact again the meaning within it. Over time, our grasp of this meaning deepens and the nourishment we draw from the symbol becomes more sustaining and satisfying.

Such a living symbol is different from a mere image. It is different even from an archetypal image. We are surrounded by these images on all sides – at the movies, in advertising, in literature. An archetypal image experienced in a movie, for example, may be profoundly moving. We may react emotionally and be led into extensive reflections on its meaning. We may think about it for days and remember it for weeks, sometimes even for years. Movies can be like dreams in this way, and certain of them remain with us for most of our lives. And yet we would not call the movie image a living symbol. A movie can affect us emotionally, but it does not transform our lives. I will not say it never can, only that it rarely does; and when compared with religious experience, the rarity seems even greater. Religions have been the carriers of living symbols for millions of people throughout time.

What every religion demands and no movie (to date, at least) has ever demanded is a meaningful sacrifice. We do not leave the movie theater and give all that we have to the poor, build cathedrals with our tithes, or devote ourselves to supporting a priestcraft. Of course, in a commercial sense, we do this as a collective, by buying tickets over and over again. But the movies keep changing. They are entertainment, and entertainment images, although they may touch the archetypal level, are not living symbols because they do not evoke a serious impulse to sacrifice the ego. The movie's voice, while heard, does not constellate the Self into a demand for ego sacrifice. The Self just does not go for it. The movie house lacks the seriousness and spiritual reality that is so fully present in the church and temple. In church, the images are not movie stars, they are realities. They therefore constellate reality in us, and the Self responds.

It seems to me especially important in our time to make this distinction, because we are inundated with images contrived to stir us emotionally and give us a thrill, a high, or a shudder. We are playing with what the ancients considered the *numinosum*, deploying these energies for ulterior – i.e., ego – purposes, such as making money or gaining fame and recognition. The element of sacrifice is entirely lacking on the part of those who play the roles, and therefore what is communicated is cynical: the psyche is merely the ego's playground. This playground is our modern glory and our spiritual desert. In the end, the Self is silent, the center is empty, and the human spirit is destitute. What can be done?

Sacrifice the horse.

"And now he had to use his own legs, and when he had walked a long way, he came to a large city. . . ."

## PART III: ARCHETYPES AND ANGELS

Let me summarize what I have been saying so far before going on to investigate the rest of our story. The great stories of the world, among which I include the Bible and "The White Snake," do not get used up but continue to yield more and more insights the more they are probed and explored. This is because they contain symbols, which connect our egos to the depths of the unconscious, the archetypes, and ultimately even the Self. These stories are themselves potentially our "white snakes," in that they are able, if we ingest them, to open our ears to the language of the archetypes. They teach us about the "things of God," the things that lie beyond our conscious limitations. This is because their authors were "inspired": they were led to these images and themes by the *spiritus rector*, just as individually we are led to images by our dream-maker. The great stories can open our ears to the languages of the animals and the angels. But we must eat of them, read them deeply and with energy.

When a story connects us in this way to the depths and leads us to the Self, the Self responds by enacting a sacrifice upon the ego. Every experience of the Self, Jung wrote, is a defeat for the ego. This comes about spontaneously, as in our story: the act of sacrifice is made spontaneously, without calculation or forethought. It is not an expiation or a propitiation—types of sacrifice that are generally directed by the ego and guided by the ego's anxiety about punishment from above, from the gods. In this case, rather, the Self spontaneously manifests, and the ego must deliver itself over to sacrifice whether it wants to or not. This spontaneous sacrifice is a sure sign that the Self has been reached and has moved into action. This is the Self's way of beginning the movement toward incarnation, toward manifestation within the ego world. A spontaneous and perhaps foolish-looking ego sacrifice is demanded and made.

Returning to our story, we see that our hero has indeed become open to the unconscious and that the Self has been moved. The preparations have been laid down for the hero's individuation. In the remainder of this investigation I will discuss his individuation process, outlining what is a common, archetypally structured process belonging properly to the second half of life.

In other words, I take our hero to be on the other side of the midlife divide, and so I do not refer to him as a "young man." I think of him as considerably advanced in age and maturity, and if the text refers to him as young that is only because he is young in spirit, as are all who individuate. An eighty- or ninety-five-year-old person who is individuating is "young," too.

As our hero enters the great city on foot, he hears a great hue and cry in the streets. An official is riding up and down announcing that the king's daughter is ready to marry and that she will marry any suitor who can perform the hard task set for him by the king, her father. But he also learns that many have tried and the price for failure is death. Nevertheless, when he sees the princess he is so smitten by her beauty that he forgets the cost and applies to the king for a chance to win her hand.

So begins the third part of this tightly packed fairy tale. In the first part the hero, then the servant of a wise king, gained knowledge of the unconscious (the "language of the animals") by breaking the rule and tasting the flesh of the white snake. This led him to separate from the king and venture out into the world on his own. This was the start of his individuation process, and he was well prepared for it by his encounter with the white snake.

In the second part of the story, he exercises compassion for the animals, whose language he understands, and he demonstrates his sensitivity to inner and outer worlds surrounding his ego consciousness. By doing so he also forges alliances with the forces in the wider world, and they promise to pay back his favors: "One good turn deserves another!" This part of the story culminates in the hero's killing his horse for the fledgling ravens, an extraordinary gesture of sacrifice in which he demonstrates his ability and willingness to put his ego aside for the sake of spiritual growth and future possibility. In these gestures of sacrifice, he shows his strong commitment to follow the call of individuation. But the sacrifices also lift him into another realm of existence, where he will be given the opportunity to win the soul, his anima, the princess. This winning of the soul is the masterpiece of individuation according to Jung.

Before reflecting upon the tasks and challenges set by the princess and the king, I would like to pause for a moment and think about the hero's character as revealed by the story so far, as well as about our relation to and feelings about him. Above all we have to recognize that this is a character who is capable of individuating. We know this because he is able to make the spontaneous movements and gestures that allow individuation to proceed. He can break the taboo and eat of the white snake; he can get down off his high horse and sacrifice him for the sake of the fledgling ravens; he can risk his life for the chance to win the princess. In other words, he represents an ego attitude free of the restrictions imposed by the complexes that thwart attempts at individuation. He can go all out.

Most of us are not free enough to individuate fully. We can do it a little perhaps, but our sense of duty and responsibility to authority restricts us: we cannot break the rules and put ourselves on a par with the king and eat the white snake. We cannot free ourselves enough from the constraints of the superego to experience the unconscious. We are too "good" (in the conventional sense) to individuate, which means we are too bound up by unspoken rules and regulations. These are mostly imposed and reinforced from within ourselves through the parental complexes (Freud's "superego"), which threaten us with guilt and punishment if we even think of delving into our own inner life genuinely and deeply. We are bound by superego constraints. A sacrifice made from such an attitude is an expiation of sin or a propitiation to the threatening parental gods.

If we manage to get over this hurdle, we are blocked by what I would call "common sense." Common sense is the consensual view of reality, what "anybody in his right mind" would say and do in similar circumstances; nothing too extreme. Common sense can certainly be a blessing and even a virtue, since it keeps us from lurching off on dangerous highways and byways. But it can also be a binder, an inhibitor, something that prevents individuation. There comes a moment when everything must be thrown into the balance and you have to go all-out, and it is usually a moment that hardly anyone else would recognize or agree with: a divorce, a job change, a move. This moment demands that common sense be transcended, that the horse be sacrificed for the little black birds, for some new possibilities, for a new future. And if this extreme violation of the rule of common sense cannot be achieved at this particular moment, individuation will be limited and at a later point may fail. What needs to be transcended in this moment is the ego complex's anxiety about survival. Imagine a person who has lost a fortune being asked by a street person for a handout and giving him the last ten dollars in his pocket. This is the highest test of the capacity for individuation: can the Self be trusted enough in this moment to risk ego-annihilation and starvation? Here the issue is basic trust in the Self.

Two qualities necessary for full individuation, then, are a) one's ego's ability to override the parental complexes, the superego, for the sake of experiencing the unconscious directly for oneself, and b) one's ability to trust the Self enough for basic survival, so that one can sacrifice one's ease and comfort and risk an extreme sacrifice that violates the rules of common sense.

A third quality that is necessary if individuation is to take place fully and completely is demonstrated when our hero falls in love with the princess simply at the sight of her. Interpreting the story on an extraverted interpersonal level, this would indicate his psyche's ability to project the anima out into the world. Interpreting it on the intrapsychic level, it has to do with the ability to respond with love and desire to an image of the soul as presented in a dream or vision, a sort of inner projection of the anima. In the latter case, one might become a monk or a nun or a Dante. Either way it means the hero can make a full-hearted and complete response to beauty, to the soul, to the "other" who embodies his or her missing part and without whom life would not be complete. One is able to break out of the shell of egohood and fall in love. This openness to responding fully to the soul is a third requisite for individuation, and it also represents ego-transcendence: for the sake of winning the other, one will risk one's own life.

This extraordinary freedom from fear and from restriction by the inner demons that we call complexes is what makes the hero of this story so remarkable and so admirable to us. And we admire and love him so much (at least I do) precisely because he can do what we cannot, what we dare not. He represents an ideal ego, not because of his purity and virtue, as with Parsifal, nor because of his prowess, as with the Greek heroes Hercules and Achilles, but because he is ideally free of the fears and pressures that inhibit most of us from individuating fully. He is like Buddha, who gives up his kingdom and goes forth with a begging bowl and sits stubbornly under a tree waiting for enlightenment, or like Jesus, who breaks the rules, violates common sense, and risks all for his inner calling and love. There is a freedom here from the parental complexes and from ego-anxieties about survival, as well as a willingness to pursue the inner imperative and love to the utmost. For most of us this kind of a figure is compensatory to our own limited attempts at individuation. He functions like a dream ego, who can do what I cannot do in waking life, and in this way encourages me to do a bit more, to venture a little further, to risk something I might not otherwise be inclined to risk. The dream ego is often several steps ahead of the waking ego (cf. Dieckmann 1991, pp. 112ff.) and leads it forward, preparing the way. This is what the story of Jesus has done for millions of Christians over the last twenty centuries, what the life of Buddha has done for millions of Buddhists for even longer, and what our dreams can do for all of us on a daily basis if we follow them. The human capacity for full individuation is represented in these figures, and if we meditate on them and let them teach us, they will help us overcome some of our inner resistances to individuation. This is the therapeutic function of myth and story and dream.

Stories like "The White Snake" can also teach us something about the nature of full individuation. What does it look like? When the hero enters the realm of the new king – now on foot, having sacrificed his horse – he is entering into a new and unfamiliar dimension of existence. In this realm it is possible for commoners to court the king's daughter and win the inheritance that comes with her. In other words, this is a place where full individuation is possible. Had the hero stayed in the first realm, the most he could have hoped for would have been to become the greatest among the servants of the king. In this new realm he himself can be elevated to kingship: he can become completely fulfilled, completely actualized, fully individuated. The usually rigid boundary between commoner and royalty is permeable here, and this means, in traditional understandings of the nature of kingship, that a common mortal ego can become like God. For the king is akin to if not identical with the Deity, and to be "royal" is to be included among the immortals. From a psychological point of view, the hero has entered a realm and an aspect of individuation where the archetypal world has become accessible to the ego and the boundaries between the personal and the collective psyches are extremely fluid. It is realm where the literal and the symbolic can get together and marry, where ego and anima/animus can unite permanently.

The danger in this realm, as we know from clinical experience and everyday observation, is inflation. The ego can become identified with an archetype and lose its identity; it can become God Almighty, inflated with grandiosity and self-importance, entitled, narcissistically bloated, and generally pretty difficult to be around – if not downright dangerous. When an ego becomes inflated, reality-testing becomes problematic because the inflated ego does not recognize boundaries and limitations like mortality; it has become divine and godlike and sees all the rules of normal living as meant for others but not for oneself. This ego becomes confused in a world of fantasy and grows exceedingly unrealistic and grandiose. It has not transcended common sense – it has lost it!

Because the risk of inflation is so great here, our story provides several tests. These will determine whether or not our hero is truly qualified to become fully individuated, to marry the princess and become king himself. If he fails the tests, he will be rejected; if he passes them, he can assume the position of prince consort and eventually, king of the realm. As king he will represent the Self, and to his subjects he will be a deity. As this is a great and a treacherous responsibility, great care must be taken in his selection.

The king administers the first test. He throws a ring into the sea and tells the suitor that he must fetch it up from the bottom and that he will be thrown back into the water until he does so or drowns. It is a harsh and difficult test, and as the suitor stands on the shore pondering what to do, the people shake their heads sadly and walk away, leaving him alone. But before the hero even enters the water, the fish he has saved earlier come to the surface and drop the ring at his feet. He is saved and, more than that, can now present himself to the king as the first successful suitor.

What is this test about, what does it mean, and why is it important for individuation? If we take the point of view that the ego is being tested by the Self here, the question to be answered is this: Is your connection with the unconscious (symbolized by the sea and the fish) good enough so that you can form and sustain a relationship (symbolized by the ring) with the anima (symbolized by the princess)? Our hero passes with flying colors. He has an excellent relationship with the unconscious; we saw him forging it in the earlier part of the story, and now the unconscious is willing to cooperate with him as he pursues his individuation goal. He is able to make a commitment to a relationship and keep it. He can stay related, and this will help to prevent inflation later if he wins the prize. The individuating ego must be able to stay related, otherwise it loses touch with the polarities in the Self. It becomes too one-sided, and the energy derived from its contact with the archetypes gets used for purely egoistic ends. Such a king would want only to be mirrored, to hear only good news. The ring symbolizes the ability to relate to the opposite within and without, and to stay related. In this, the hero is supported by the depths of his unconscious; he does not have to do it all on his ego strength alone, by sheer will power. The inner support for relationship is there.

The suitor rejoices, thinking he has finished with the tests. He presents himself and the ring to the king, expecting to collect his reward. But now the princess intervenes. She is not satisfied. After all, he is not her equal in birth, so he must prove himself some more. She too is helping to prevent inflation on his part: Let's not make this too easy for him or it will go to his head and he will be impossible to live with. So she devises another hard test. This time the hero has to gather up all the grains from the ten sacks of millet that she has strewn around the garden. What is more, this must be done in the dark, at night. If the first task was difficult, this one looks impossible. Again, the suitor does nothing to solve the problem himself but only sits there and waits out the night. In the meantime the ants, whose king the hero honored earlier by steering his horse off the path, have come and done the work. Once again his life is saved and he qualifies for the hand of the princess.

What can we say about this test with respect to qualifying for individuation? The question here is whether the ego is in touch with the ant king—that is, the principle of hard work required of a king, the daily round of tasks and boring routines, the patience needed to govern millions of subjects, the leadership to organize masses of people and get them to work together. This is what is required of a good king. Kingship is not only a position of privilege and power; it must be grounded in a sense of responsibility and hard work. All of this is represented by the ant king. So the princess' question to the man who aspires to her hand and eventually the throne is: Are you sufficiently in touch with the ant king principle not to get inflated by marriage to me and your position as prince consort and, eventually, king? This is a question about the ego's tenacity and core strength, its ability to resist letting grandiose fantasies take over. It is akin to Jesus' test in the wilderness, when he was tempted by Satan with power and worldly glory. Would he pass or fail the test of grandiosity and inflation? Again our young hero passes the test. He is sufficiently in contact with the ant king.

Yet even this success does not conquer the proud heart of the princess. Why is she so difficult to win? One could attempt to psychoanalyze her: she has an overdeveloped positive father complex and cannot bear to make the transition to another man. It is an oedipal bond too strong to be broken by a mere mortal man, a commoner. But since I am looking at the fairy tale from the hero's point of view, I am inclined to see the princess' pride and stubbornness rather as a test of the ego's mettle. Is the suitor strong and determined enough to endure the trials set before him to win the prize of soul? Does he have the stuff for full individuation? The soul is not easily won, as anyone who has set his heart on winning her can testify. She is proud, she is ruthless, and the tests put to the ego are endless. Our hero has to face only three tests, which in symbolic language signal a complete cycle. In life as we know it, there are multitudinous trials before the symbolic number three, or culmination, is reached.

Thus the princess proposes a third task. If the suitor is to have her hand in marriage, he must bring her an apple from the Tree of Life. Sadly, for he does not know where to look, the hero sets out to find the Tree, ultimately wandering through three kingdoms in his search. We must note in passing that, although he is neither a passive fellow nor one inclined to give up in despair even if the task seems hopeless, he could not have accomplished even one of the tasks set before him with his conscious knowledge and strength alone. So he comes to a point where he lies down under a tree to sleep, and there the solution comes to him. He hears a rustling in the branches and a golden apple falls into his hand. Three ravens, the very ones he had fed earlier upon the flesh of his own horse, appear and tell him that they have remembered their debt to him: hearing about his dilemma, they had flown to the end of the world where the Tree of Life stands and fetched the apple for him. Now the suitor knows he has won the princess, and when he presents the golden apple to her, she has no more excuses to make. They cut the apple in two and eat it together, and when the princess eats of it her heart becomes filled with love for the man who won her. They live in peace and happiness to a great age.

What is this final test about? Why does the princess demand an apple from the Tree of Life, and what is this meant to prove about the suitor's qualifications? The golden apples at the end of the world seem to be a reference to the Greek myth of the Hesperides. The Hesperides were guardians of a tree of golden apples given by Gaia to Hera upon the occasion of her wedding to Zeus. The garden where the tree grew was believed to exist at the western border of the ocean. The third hard task in our story, then, refers us to the classical *hieros gamos* or sacred marriage between Hera and Zeus. Only the greatest of heroes, Heracles himself, was able to force his way past Ladon, the dragon who guarded the tree, and take some apples away. Because these apples were golden, they also symbolized immortality.

In our tale, this reference to the classical golden apples of the Hesperides is mixed in with a reference to the biblical myth of the Garden of Eden: the apples come from the Tree of Life. The Tree of Life, according to Genesis 2:9, stands in the center of the Garden of Eden and symbolizes the fullness of the creation. It is also a symbol of the hope for fulfillment at the end of time: "To him who conquers I will grant to eat of the Tree of Life, which is in the paradise of God" (Revelation 2:7), and "Then he showed me the river of the water of life, bright as crystal, flowing from the throne of God and of the Lamb through the middle of the street of the city; also, on either side of the river, the Tree of Life with its twelve kinds of fruit, yielding its fruit each month; and the leaves of the Tree were for the healing of the nations" (Revelation 22:1-2). In the Bible, the Tree of Life appears at the beginning and the end, in the first book and in the last book: it is alpha and omega. This reference lends a decidedly spiritual cast to the fairy tale, for if the hero can gain entry into paradise and bring back a symbol of ultimate wholeness and completion, he must be a spiritual hero of the first rank. In Christian religious thought, only Christ achieved such a feat; it is in the Eucharist that we continue to feed on the food of eternal life that he offered.

So the golden apple is a symbol of love, fullness, and completion as well as immortality. Its golden quality – contrasted with the usual red of apples portrayed in art, representing the sweetness and passion of physical love and desire – makes it a symbol of alchemical fulfillment: gold is the end product of the alchemical opus, which begins in *nigredo*. And this brings us back to the ravens.

It is not insignificant that it is the ravens who bring the golden apple to our hero. Because of their black color and loud, obtrusive ways, perhaps ravens are ambiguous symbolically. They can signify pestilence, bad luck, and death; also cruel parents, as we saw earlier in our story. But they are also associated with solar deities such as Mithras and Apollo. In relation to this story they are clearly positive, in the sense that it is through them that the hero is able to complete his mission. And it is because he forged such a strong relationship to them through his extraordinary sacrifice earlier in the story that he is able now to complete the task of individuation. So when the princess tests him with the final impossible task, it is to see whether or not he is in touch with the spiritual power to fly to the ends of the earth, enter the guarded and forbidden territory of paradise, and bring back into the here-and-now of quotidian life an effective symbol of that world. Could he approach the Self and bring some of it back into everyday life, again without being destroyed by inflation or identification with the archetype of wholeness? Is he capable of being a spiritual master? For some reason, all this is necessary if he is to win the princess. She is demanding in the extreme. She will have nothing but the ultimate. And yet we should not wonder at this, for she is the daughter of the king.

What saves the hero from hubris and inflation is the knowledge that he has not accomplished any one of these three impossible tasks by his own effort and designs. Because he is open to the unconscious and its powers – the fish, the ants, the ravens – he has the resources to individuate and to achieve wholeness. If he had performed the tasks himself, he would have cause to feel proud. Instead, all has been done "not by my will but thine." He has done what was necessary to create relationships with figures of the unconscious: he has shown empathy, he has gone out of his way for their sake, and he has sacrificed. In his need, they do not forget him: "One good turn deserves another." In this way he is protected from ego inflation.

Each of the animal helpers represents an archetypal source of energy and agency. The fish represent the hero's contact with sexuality and relationship, his ability to love and to contain that passion; the ant king and ant hoard represent his connection to directed activity, to work and diligence, and to the stable forms which that energy can achieve; and the ravens symbolize his contact with spirit, with depth and profundity, with the possibility of reaching beyond the visible world and coming into contact with the ultimate source of all that is, of energy and matter, of spirit and flesh. He does not become inflated because he does not identify with any of these helpers, nor does he claim their power to be under his ego control. He waits on them and is as surprised as anyone when they come to his aid. They are his angels.

Archetypes are angels. Just as angels come from God, represent God, are of the same substance as God, and deliver God's messages, archetypes originate in the Self, represent the Self when they appear to the ego in dream or vision or fantasy, are made up of the same psychic and extrapsychic material as the Self, and deliver the intended messages of the Self. The difference is that in psychological life we have recognized that archetypes come in many forms and images: not only as winged creatures of light but as animals and other forms as well. In our story, they appear as fish, ants, and ravens. These are the angels who assist and guide our hero on his individuation journey.

At the end of the story, the princess finally experiences love and commitment to the hero after she eats of the golden apple. The fact that they eat the apple at all seems extraordinary to me. Wouldn't you lock it up in a case or place it in a shrine? This is a golden apple from the Tree of Life! What a treasure! Something to pass on to the children! But no, they cut it in half and eat it, and it transforms the heart of the princess. This was the required final step, of course, without which the story would not have been complete, the hero's individuation would have been left hanging. They must unite in love.

Alchemical gold was noted for its ability to "tincture," that is, to transform whatever it touched into gold. This is what happens to the princess in the story's last scene. She is touched by the power of love and her heart is opened. Without this, the union would be unstable. The golden apple, and especially the act of eating it, makes the union between hero and princess as stable and durable as gold itself. Here we have an image of an ultimate *coniunctio* and one which is not followed by further adventures, ups and downs, and developments. It is itself the final and ultimate state. The gold has been achieved.

Fairy tales are commonly criticized for ending with ". . . and they lived happily ever after." This seems so unrealistic. Life is not like that. There are always further tests and trials. What happens after they have had a couple of kids and there is restlessness in the land and enemy armies attack the frontiers? And so on. Life is full of disasters, betrayals, and broken dreams.

The conclusion of this fairy tale does not, in my opinion, indicate a state that can be achieved by mortals in this life, any more than the images of final fulfillment in the Book of Revelation are meant to represent events that take place in time and space, within the context of history. The individuation process depicted symbolically in "The White Snake" points to a goal that is ultimate and final. If anything, something like it may be approximated at death. Edward Edinger speaks of death as the final and greatest *coniunctio*. Jung's own deepest *coniunctio* experiences, as described in *Memories, Dreams, Reflections* (Jung 1961, pp. 294–295), took place when he was on the verge of dying. And according to a report by Laurens van der Post, a close friend of Jung's and of his family, Jung's dream on the night before he died depicted an uprooted tree whose roots were filled with great lumps of gold.

And so this is how I read the final sentence of our tale: "They cut the Apple of Life in two and ate it together, and then her heart became full of love for him, and they lived in undisturbed happiness to a great age." It is a state of individuation fulfilled and completed to the greatest extent possible or imaginable, a state occasionally glimpsed or experienced for a moment in daily life but held steadily as a goal, the object of our hopes and deepest desires for wholeness and true value.

## REFERENCES

Dieckman, H. 1986. *Twice-Told Tales*. Wilmette, Ill.: Chiron Publications.

———. 1991. *Methods in Analytical Psychology*. Wilmette, Ill.: Chiron Publications.

Eliade, M. 1963. *Myth and Reality*. New York: Harper and Row.

Jung, C. G. 1948. The spirit Mercurius. In *CW* 13:191–250. Princeton, N.J.: Princeton University Press, 1967.

———. 1954a. Transformation symbolism in the Mass. In *CW* 11:201–296. Princeton, N.J.: Princeton University Press, 1969.

———. 1954b. On the nature of the psyche. In *CW* 8:159–234. Princeton, N.J.: Princeton University Press, 1969.

———. 1961. *Memories, Dreams, Reflections*. New York: Random House.

Meador, B. 1992. *Uncursing the Dark*. Wilmette, Ill.: Chiron Publications.

Moore, P. 1992. *No Other Gods*. Wilmette, Ill.: Chiron Publications.

Neumann, E. 1954. *The Origins and History of Consciousness*. Princeton, N.J.: Princeton University Press.

———. 1974. *The Great Mother*. Princeton, N.J.: Princeton University Press.

Samuels, A. 1989. *The Plural Psyche*. London: Routledge.

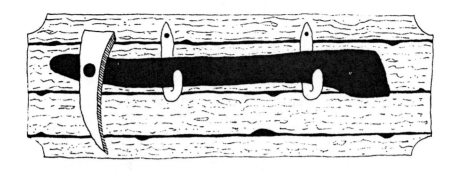

# "Clever Elsie"
# A Story of Fragmentation into Psychosis

## Lionel Corbett

This tale depicts the tragic descent of a fragile personality into a psychosis. Like all fairy tales, the story is like an x-ray of the psyche – only the bare bones of the narrative are given, so interpretation requires us to extrapolate from the merest allusions and hints. The one advantage to such extreme brevity of description is that we can assume everything that is included is really essential and no detail is irrelevant. My hermeneutic method assumes that clues from the text give us a picture of Elsie's inner world and tell us about her childhood. The weakness of this approach is that the text is so terse that the interpreter inevitably projects or imagines what the flesh around the bones may have looked like. For this purpose we must draw on two sources, namely our empathic grasp of Elsie's situation and psychodynamic or family theory. But given the inevitable limitations of treating a text as though it were a patient, the story illustrates in ways that fit remarkably well with modern understanding of the intrapsychic situation of a potential schizophrenic, the pathological interactions that occur within her family, and the way she decompensates.

## Clever Elsie

A man had a daughter called Clever Elsie. When she grew up, her father decided: "We will get her married." Her mother agreed, but with the proviso: "If only someone would come who would have her." Finally, Hans, who came from far away, said he would marry Elsie as long as she was really smart. In order to prove this point, her father reassured Hans that Elsie had plenty of good sense, and her mother told him that Elsie could see the wind and hear the flies coughing.

One day while Hans and the family were all having dinner, Elsie's mother asked her to bring up some beer from the cellar. As she went down to do so, Elsie briskly tapped the lid of the pitcher, so that the time might not appear long. Sitting down, she was very careful to avoid hurting herself in any way. While the beer was running, she would not let her eyes be idle but scanned the wall ahead, noticing a pick-axe left behind by the masons. At this, Elsie began to weep with fear. "If I get Hans and we have a child and he grows big and we send him into the cellar here to draw beer, the pick-axe will fall on his head and kill him," she thought. Then she wept and screamed at this misfortune, staying away from the table for so long that the family sent the maid to find her. When Elsie told her why she was so distraught, the maid said, "What a clever Elsie we have!" and joined Elsie in her wailing. Growing thirsty, the family then sent a boy down to find out what had happened. When Elsie repeated her lament, the boy agreed with her and all three howled together at the coming catastrophe. It was now Elsie's mother's turn to investigate the delay. Finding them all weeping inconsolably, she too was told the reason: that Elsie's future child was to be killed by the falling pick-axe. At that the mother forgot all about dinner and began to weep along with the others. Eventually, Elsie's father came downstairs; on hearing the story, he too joined in the family distress. Finding himself alone at the table, the bridegroom went down to the cellar and found them all screaming piteously, each one outdoing the other. When Elsie explained the problem, Hans realized that someone with such keen understanding was right for him and he immediately married her.

One day, after they had been together a while, Hans asked Elsie to go to the field and cut some corn for bread while he went to work. When Elsie arrived at the field, she could not decide whether to begin by working or by eating the food she had brought. She decided to eat and then to sleep before cutting the corn. Meanwhile

Hans, who was waiting for her to return, decided that she was taking so long because she was so clever and industrious that she did not even come home to eat. But by evening he decided to go and see how much corn she had cut. Finding her asleep with nothing at all done, Hans hung a fowler's net strung with little bells around her. He then returned home. Eventually Elsie awoke in total darkness and at each step heard the jingling of bells. This alarmed her to the extent that she no longer knew if she really was Clever Elsie or not, and she wondered, "Is it I or is it not I?" In great doubt and fear, she decided to go home and ask. "If it be I or if it be not I, they will be sure to know," she thought. As the door to her house was shut, she knocked on the window crying, "Hans, is Elsie within?" Hans replied that yes, Elsie was in the house. At this, Elsie became terrified, realizing that "It is not I." And so she went from house to house in the village, but no one would let her in because of the sound of the bells. Then she ran out of the village, and no one has seen her since.

## INTERPRETATION

This tale gives us a glimpse into a very pathological family system, one with very fluid boundaries. We see how Elsie has always been identified as vulnerable and different, probably because of her perceptual hyperawareness. This excessive sensitivity has allowed the family to scapegoat her to the extent that she eventually loses the battle for sanity or psychic survival. Burdened with her overarousal and her family difficulties, Elsie survives until the threats of marriage and leaving home appear. Terrified by the prospect of separation and by the memories and feelings stimulated by the thought of having a child, Elsie initially tries to hold herself together with obsessional and paranoid defenses. These defenses finally break down, and she is driven mad as her tenuous sense of self dissolves under her narcissistic husband's enraged, sadistic invalidation of her precarious sense of reality.

My intention in the elucidation of this story is to suggest a theory of the origin of psychosis based on a synthesis of Jungian and psychoanalytic notions.

### The Initial Problem: Elsie's Biological Vulnerability

The story begins with the implication that something in the family is skewed; Elsie has two parents, but it is as if she belongs only to her father and not her mother. It also seems that there must be something terribly wrong with her, since no marriage will occur unless her parents actively arrange it. Her mother is doubtful that anyone who knows Elsie would want to marry her. Indeed, Elsie's mother's sarcasm and despair carry a tone of envy or hatred, perhaps because Elsie is primarily her father's daughter. We hear this mocking tone in the spiteful epithet *clever*, a word that seems to carry a sinister meaning in this case. It obviously does not refer to Elsie's intelligence but to an extraordinary hyperacuity of sensation that enables her to "see" the wind and "hear" the flies coughing. The role of this kind of perceptual difficulty in the life of the schizophrenic is well known (Corbett 1976). We can only guess at the sensitivity of Elsie's other senses, but it seems that she lives in a state of intense perceptual overstimulation and hyperarousal; ordinary levels of sound and light must seem incredibly intense to her. Imagine Elsie as a baby, attempting to protect herself from a barrage of sound and light. All she can do is turn away, withdraw, or try to sleep. Closing her eyes will help, but sound is difficult to shut out for a baby, making ordinary levels of household noise seem like claps of thunder. Further, we can imagine what it must be like for this extraordinarily sensitive baby to be handled by adults – the level of intrusion must be terrifying. To understand how this problem might affect her relationships with her parents, we might turn to recent theories describing the mutual influence of mother and child. Mother-infant interactions in the first part of life are critical in the development of intrapsychic structures. I use this term in a way that is synonymous with *complexes* in the Jungian sense, that is, enduring configurations or patterns of affect, behavior, and perception formed by the interaction of the child's archetypal endowment with his or her caregivers. Mother and child are a unit, and experiences which happen between them belong to the system rather than the individual. Each participant therefore influences the other, creating patterns of mutual regulation (Beebe and Lachman 1988), and these patterns help to form self- and other representations that are then incorporated into complexes. Elsie's need to protect herself from excessive stimulation would severely limit her attempts to respond to her parents, and her withdrawal from her parents' ordinary attempts to engage her would make her a most unsatisfying baby to care for. Ideally, each person in the parent-child dyad needs to be able to match the other in order to enter his or her perceptual and affective world. However, because of her hyperawareness, Elsie probably has been more concerned to avoid than to match her parents' interactions with her. Perhaps this has happened to a degree that they could not understand, because she experienced their approaches as so intense as to be intrusive or persecutory. With a difficult baby such as Elsie, parent-child interactions eventually become hopelessly misattuned and bonding fails. One therefore suspects that an early and mutual estrangement must have taken place, worse for her mother than for her father. Her mother must have missed the normal rewards of interacting with an emotionally responsive infant. Thus Elsie can be seen to have started life in a frightening, lonely, and painfully overstimulating world. It is in this context that we have to understand her subsequent intrapsychic difficulties and her interaction with her family. We should also remember that mutual influence theory prevents an excessive blaming of her parents by acknowledging the child's contribution.

Elsie's hypersensitivity to the environment is presumably a biological endowment, the somatic pole of an archetypal ability to perceive stimuli imperceptible to others. Thus we may infer that she has a corresponding psychic sensitivity and that the two together predispose her to develop severe psychopathology because of early interactive difficulties. Elsie's organic difficulty underpins and helps to clarify much of what happens to her. Lest we forget that the archetype expresses itself somatically (in this case via the brain) as well as via the psyche, the neurological aspect of her problem is worth some attention. It has long been established that schizophrenics have hyperarousable and hyperlabile nervous systems. They cannot properly modulate excitation (Epstein and Coleman 1970) and so are vulnerable to emotional overload. As a result they are overly affected by stress, from which they recover slowly. They are particularly reactive to anxiety (Mednick 1958), especially in the presence of personal censure (Rodnick 1973). The high level of arousal attached to their inner world makes it difficult for them to distinguish the source of a percept or thought, so that they cannot easily distinguish between inside and outside (Maier 1956). Imagery and feelings are so intense that they may be felt to come from without, and the boundaries of the self are accordingly unclear. All of the biological work in this field can be summarized by saying that schizophrenics become disorganized easily when they are overloaded with anxiety-provoking stimuli. Bearing in mind this burden that Elsie has to carry, we may now return to the family and the psychodynamic milieu in which her biological vulnerability has unfolded, producing her eventual psychotic fragmentation.

## Elsie's Family

The family's choice for Elsie of the sarcastic description *clever* may have been the result of her emotional oddity. This seems to be the case because everyone calls her clever at the very moment that she is terrified by her catastrophic fantasies of the death of her child. She screams that this will happen "if I get Hans," suggesting an almost clairvoyant ability to intuitively read the future, based, I suspect, on her sensitivity to the unconsciouses of those around her. Her sensitivity to the subtleties of her parents' behavior, especially of their unconsciouses, would have made them uncomfortable, and may have led them to retaliate via the sarcastic nickname. Perhaps Elsie's parents are the type of very brittle people who need to maintain a particular world view or rigorously defended perception of themselves and cannot tolerate a child who perceives things differently or points out what has been swept under the rug. Her parents' need to defend against their own vulnerability may have forced Elsie to deny her own acute and unusual perception of reality in order to maintain a connection with them — after all, they are all she has. In such families, children typically orient themselves according to their parents' need to maintain their own emotional equilibrium. In the process a child who has to distort her own feelings and perception (Lidz 1973) cannot develop a reliable and consistent picture of the world around her (Searles 1965). This sacrifice, of course, makes it hard for the child to develop a separate sense of self; she becomes too adaptive, too sensitive to the needs of others. This may be why, when the story tells us the parents are eager for Hans to marry Elsie, it does not suggest that Elsie was even consulted in the matter.

Hans' stipulation that Elsie be "really smart" in order for him to marry her is revealing. It seems that he is not interested in her for her own sake, rather he expects that her smartness will enhance him in some way. He thus makes her connection to him conditional, and indeed Elsie suffers terribly when, because of his rage at her perceived failure, he totally severs their bond. This kind of situation in marriage is usually a repeat of an early situation with a parent and may be additional evidence that Elsie has always been held hostage to the ruthless needs of another. We shall see that her very selfhood depends on maintaining this connection.

### The Courtship: Elsie's Anxiety

Elsie must be very frightened at the prospect of marriage. We can imagine how this prospect stimulates her fears of separation from the only relationships she has and of engulfment by the egocentric Hans. Her fear of sexuality must also be intense because of her low tolerance for intrusion. Elsie's high level of anxiety is first seen when her mother sends her downstairs for beer. (It seems odd that the maid is not sent first—perhaps this indicates Elsie's low status in the household.) Elsie tries to bind or contain her anxiety as she descends the cellar stairs by tapping the lid of the pitcher, "so that the time might not appear long." This comment suggests that her perceptual difficulties include difficulty with the perception of time. Piaget (1969) points out that the child's sense of time is related to the expectation that her needs will be satisfied. The infant's ability to depend upon and predict her environment, which requires time perception, is important in the development of reality testing. The baby can only perceive time as a sequence in the presence of a mother who is reasonably consistent and predictable. Accordingly, difficulties in the differentiation of self and object also lead to difficulties in the development of a sense of time (Blatt 1976). The schizophrenic is typically temporally disorganized, and the severity of this problem is related to the degree to which reality testing is impaired (Obendorf 1941). The story also captures movingly Elsie's sense of personal frailty by stressing how carefully she sits before the beer barrel, without stooping or "doing herself any unexpected injury." She is unable to move with abandon, perhaps because her body does not feel entirely real or because she feels its fragility or because of unpleasantly intense interoceptive stimulation.

### The Onset of Her Terror: The Pick-Axe

While the beer is running Elsie is apparently unable to relax. Instead, she is hypervigilant, which suggests that she needs (perhaps habitually) to scan her environment for signs of danger. Speculatively, sitting in front of a keg of beer might add to her anxiety if alcohol is a problem in her family. It is noteworthy that Elsie singles out a pick-axe as the focus of her fear. I have the strong sense that her associations are that she is about to be axed or otherwise brutally penetrated. She knows that Hans has an axe to grind and that her parents have made him promises that she has to live up to, so that this marriage will repeat the demand that she submit. Overall, the axe stirs up Elsie's infantile experiences of being too open to attack. She imagines sex with Hans, then having a child who in her fantasy represents herself, especially as she is in this regressed and terrified state of mind. In her fantasy, she/the child is killed by this axe. The image of the death of the child rapidly escalates to become an obsessional rumination reminiscent of those painful thoughts mothers have, which contain an unconscious death wish toward their child. We cannot help wondering if this all occurs because, as a child, Elsie "picked up" her mother's death wish toward her. It is hard to imagine the return of a more terrifying repressed event.

### The Family Merger

As each member of the family finds Elsie in her distress, it is striking that no one tries to reassure her or inject any reality testing into her catastrophic thinking. Although she seems a prime candidate for simple cognitive therapy, the others only join her in her lamentations. It is as if the family is unable to form boundaries between individual members (Lidz 1973). The ready way in which the family enters Elsie's inner world actually reinforces her irrational fears. This is not a healthy affirmation of a child by her parents but a pseudoconfirmation that actually intensifies her difficulty. If this pattern is typical, the family must have been of little help to Elsie during her development, especially in teaching her the skills of self-soothing and reality testing. It is difficult to tell if the scene of them all wailing by the beer barrel is really a *folie en famille*, in which they all actually believe Elsie, or simply a sadistic reinforcement of her pain. Similarly, it is hard to tell if Hans's acceptance of her manifest pathology as proof of her "cleverness" is to be taken literally or as a bizzare and cruel joke, only the beginning of his psychological terrorism toward Elsie, which culminates in his driving her out of her precariously balanced mind.

For heuristic purposes, I assume that the scene of the family merged together in a single, as it were, unified field of consciousness represents a typical interactive pattern and is both involuntary and unconscious. The story's depiction of the entire family all participating in Elsie's lament about a disaster that has not happened is then clear evidence of the lack of boundaries with which she grew up. This situation is likely to have been another pathogenic influence adding to Elsie's neurological difficulty. Boundary formation is developmentally fundamental, and the blurring of boundaries is a core problem in the families of schizophrenics (Blatt and Wild 1976). Assuming that this tendency toward merger and lack of differentiation between herself and others has been the situation since birth, one can imagine how unstable and poorly defined Elsie's representational world must be with regard to her sense of self in relation to others. The sense of self as separate and the experience of others as apart from oneself seem to be interdependent (ibid.). If there is inadequate self/other differentiation internally, the development of a clear boundary between oneself and the outer world is also impaired. The kind of fusion problem Elsie experiences with her family in the cellar contributes to the schizophrenic's difficulty distinguishing inside from outside, or self from not-self. The family's tendency to merge, in the way the story depicts, must add to Elsie's difficulty in reality testing, which is already uncertain because of her biologically based perceptual difficulty. Separation is so forbidden in Elsie's family that none of them can have their own thoughts and feelings but must share even patently absurd states of mind. The usual explanation for this kind of lack of differentiation within families is that it protects against the awareness and expression of anger (Searles 1965). All of this must render Elsie vulnerable to the total dissolution of self in the absence of connection to others, as we see in her final, awful disintegration. Separate from others, Elsie does not have the internal structures that can take over for the outer structure provided by the family.

Elsie's Loss of Self

In the last vignette of the marriage, we see that Hans wants Elsie to work at the same time as he does. But when she goes to the corn field, she decides to take care of herself first and falls asleep. What follows is a metaphor for the disaster that befalls her when she is not totally compliant with the wishes of others; Elsie cannot be sure that she even exists without validation from others because her sense of self is so unstable. Therefore she is also unable to tolerate conflict without losing herself — a sign that she was unable to introject any of the maternal holding that normally would protect one against the fear that conflict will disrupt a relationship. Hans is enraged that Elsie has not met his expectations, so he hangs a net of the kind used to catch birds around her and leaves her alone. This implies that he regards her as a bird, ungrounded and flighty, rather than as hard-working like himself; he insists that she be like him and cannot tolerate her attempt at autonomy. More can be said about this dynamic.

Hans's behavior is totally ungiving and domineering, and Elsie cannot hold her ground against him. Perhaps he is the kind of man who tries to control others in order to defend against his personal fragility. Without the reassurance that such control brings, he feels threatened and so becomes narcissistically enraged. It is not hard to see why Elsie should have married such a man. Her relationship with Hans presumably repeats a typical pattern in the families of schizophrenics, especially women, described by Lidz (1973) as "schizmatic." In these situations, a rigid father unrealistically insists that his wife and daughter conform to his view of the world. His wife, usually herself a deprived child, is disorganized and unable to provide her daughter with any maternal warmth. Usually the wife herself was unwanted because she was a girl, and her depreciatory attitude toward her daughter reflects her attitude toward herself, leading to inevitable difficulties with her daughter's female identification. It is not unusual for fathers in such families to be both highly inconsistent and at the same time highly punitive, so that their daughters are both fearful and confused as to how to win their affection. Usually the parents are in chronic conflict, and the child tries to bridge the gap between them by offering herself as a scapegoat, appearing to be the cause of the family problem in order to obscure the real difficulty. Since Elsie has lived her life trying to protect others and see the world their way, she is really in no position to depart from Hans' wish for her to work, and her decision to eat and sleep is a form of psychological suicide.

### The Breakdown

When Elsie awakes in the darkness she hears the sound of bells all around her, which move as she moves and must be terrifyingly loud and disorienting. This alarms her because, as we have seen, Elsie has a limited capacity to test reality independently. In the dark, without anyone to orient her perceptually, she loses all her bearings. She has no idea if the bells are real or figments of her imagination, and her constant fear of insanity surfaces. Elsie now experiences her core terror—the threat of the dissolution of herself. She rushes home, desperately needing confirmation that she exists. At this point, Hans could probably have saved her by calming her down and reassuring her that she is indeed Elsie. Instead what he does is to repeat many earlier experiences of invalidation. Because of his own rage at her, he lies in a way that convinces her that his version of reality is correct, so that she realizes she does not know who she is; if he is correct, she must be wrong. To use the metaphor of the story, there is nobody home.

## A JUNGIAN VIEW OF ELSIE'S PSYCHOSIS

I would like to suggest that the usual Jungian view of psychosis is not adequate to explain what happens to Elsie. Traditionally, psychosis is viewed as a process in which the ego is overwhelmed by an eruption from the depth of the unconscious. The conscious personality is then thought to become dominated by one or more particular complexes to the extent that the personality is possessed by unintegrated, or unmediated, archetypal forces. However, in this story such a scenario is insufficient to explain Elsie's fragmentation. I believe that the classical theory actually describes a later stage of the disorder than we see here and does not really account for its onset. The presence in consciousness of the type of unmediated archetypal material described by Perry (1973) may not be the cause of the fragmentation. Rather, the appearance of this material may be the result of a more fundamental difficulty that creates a vacuum in the personal sphere and thus invites raw archetypal elements to fill the gap. Elsie's disturbance has not progressed to the degree that we see the classical picture; we are present at the initial opening of the door to the unconscious, and the problem is to understand what has opened the door too widely. At this stage we can only imagine what will emerge, and we do not know what form the restitutive processes might eventually take. Accordingly, rather than focus on such later developments, it is useful to examine how Jungian theory might cast additional light on the early processes of personality disruption, apart from those psychodynamic mechanisms already cited. In particular, what exactly has happened to Elsie's usual ego when she pathetically wails, "It is not I"? If indeed "it" is not "I," what is happening? Exactly what is it that Elsie no longer has? To suggest that her ego has been assimilated by or is identified with the unconscious, which might be part of the classical explanation, explains nothing. These are only alternative ways of describing psychosis and offer no sense of the mechanisms involved. In addition, if, as I believe, the ego cannot be taken for granted but is a structure that itself needs explaining, it is then not legitimate to use the ego as an explanatory principle. The ego is too often reified as if it were a homunculus inside the head with a steering wheel and a brake, guiding the personality. This kind of explanation explains nothing; what is it that steers the homunculus?

Here it is important to distinguish Jung's view from the standard psychoanalytic definition of ego. Jung's equation of ego with the contents of consciousness is an entirely different usage than that found in the Freudian literature, where *ego* refers to both a subdivision of the mental apparatus and to a set of intrapsychic functions. Within psychoanalysis the use of the term *ego* to simply mean the person is now being replaced by the term *self*, which, by avoiding the usual contrast of ego with id and superego, avoids any implication of a simplistic drive-defense psychology. But Jung's ego has always avoided this difficulty; it is simply the consciousness of a separate, self-reflexive sense of self, an agency distinct from others. I believe that the ego can be thought of as a learned narrative, a story of who "I" am based on all the things that have happened to me. All of this information is held together by the operation of memory, a brain function that I believe represents a part of what Jung refers to as the "somatic" basis of the ego. Jung (1951, par. 1) defines the ego as that complex which includes all psychic contents that are within or "rest on" the total field of consciousness. But he stresses that the ego does not consist of consciousness (ibid., par. 5). To my mind this correctly distinguishes between the contents of consciousness, which we can understand, and consciousness itself, which is still an insoluble problem. Elsie is still conscious, but the contents of her consciousness are no longer organized coherently into a distinct sense of self. The metaphor that comes to mind to clarify this situation is that of a shoal of fish in water. It is as if the Self, understood as the irreducible, total matrix of consciousness, is like the ocean while individual contents of the psyche are like fish swimming within it. They may be near the surface or quite deep. Normally, within the personal sphere, each content of consciousness – be it a thought, feeling, memory, idea, or image – is linked to other related contents, which are then grouped as complexes around common themes and act as relatively permanent structures. These structures move with varying degrees of unison, like orderly shoals of fish on the same general course. By a simple process of conditioning based on pleasure and pain, some contents of the psyche have learned to swim together while excluding, or being ignorant of, others. The ego therefore represents those structures of consciousness that are conditioned and conditional, possessing temporal continuity. They are not necessarily in touch with the other contents of the larger sea in which they swim. What we call the personal psyche is therefore a particular, discrete collection of these structures, which behave as enduring intrapsychic processes, more or less in harmony with each other. In the neurotic, these complexes may be swimming in opposite directions or disturbing the water with their intensity. But in the case of Elsie, the fish are simply swimming randomly and chaotically within the sea of consciousness. Elsie is therefore flooded by uncontained painful affects; her thinking and perceptual processes are unreliable and disorganized, and there is no center that can call itself "I" as if speaking for the whole person. Elsie's problem can therefore be seen not as an eruption from the depths but as a splintering or dissolution of her sense of structured, conscious separateness. It is in this area – the loss of her discrete humanness – that explanation is needed.

Elsie is especially prone to such fragmentation; "Elsie" as a truly separate entity was never fully born out of the Self, or the totality of consciousness, because her parents refused to assist with the differentiation this birth would require. This happened because she was too different for them to tolerate – they needed her to be like them or to constantly reinforce their own view of things so that they could hold their own fragile selves together. As a result, in terms of classical Jungian theory the parental complex that contributes to her final *solutio* is one that denies Elsie any sense of separateness. Elsie's fragmentation represents a redissolving of her barely nascent ego back into the totality of the consciousness of the Self. Mythically, this situation corresponds to images of children either being prevented from being born or being eaten as soon as they are born.

At this point it is evident that I have been postponing addressing the obvious question: What is the nature of the disruption that has 'unglued' the structures of Elsie's personality to the point of chaos? Jungian theory holds that the archetypes normally structure the complexes so that psychic contents that belong together stay together, in the sway of the archetype whose potential they fill. The archetypes are therefore the morphogenetic, or structure-building, principles within the psyche. To continue the metaphor, they represent lines of force moving through the water, akin to magnetic fields, that attract material of a certain quality. What catastrophe could break up these structures so that their contents move randomly? Our task is to explain how archetypal forces are allowed to dominate consciousness when none of their usual human coverings are in place. In the psychotic, it is as if the normal human shell of the complexes, which surround their archetypal centers, have exploded, exposing their transpersonal cores. The dissolution of their human elements allows archetypal material to flood consciousness, leading to delusions and hallucinations. In contrast to classical theory, I suggest that this intrusion is secondary, not the primary problem. I believe that the fundamental cause is a catastrophic disconnection of the archetypal and the human due to the failure in Elsie's primary relationships. Elsie lacks what the alchemists referred to as the *glutinum mundi*, the "glue of the world," which is the "medium between mind and body and the union of both" (Jung 1944, par. 209). The nature of this glue is further accessible to analysis.

Edinger (1985) notes that the *glutinum mundi* is an essential constituent of the *coniunctio*, and I suggest that this is exactly what has failed in Elsie's case. The *coniunctio* is an archetypal image of what Kohut (1971) refers to in personalistic or human terms as the "selfobject" relationship. A selfobject in his sense (which is different from Fordham's) is a person who has the effect of strengthening one's personal self, increasing its vitality and cohesiveness, and supplying what is missing for the wholeness of the self. The child's selfobject needs are specific archetypal "deintegrates" of the Self (Corbett 1989), that, once they unfold, require human responsiveness and mediation. They include the need for affirmation, perceptual validation, affective attunement, soothing, sameness, and belonging. The sense of a personal self is made up of the accretion and internalization of innumerable such selfobject experiences in childhood. To the extent that the selfobject milieu is defective, the personal self that results will be fragile and prone to disintegration. In Jungian terms, the archetypal needs of the Self are then not adequately humanized into firmly connected, positively toned complexes, which would normally have cohered so as to afford Elsie a strongly established personality. Instead, her parents have obviously been very poor selfobjects. Their responsiveness to Elsie's selfobject needs has been so inadequate that they do not affirm her selfhood or her perceptual reality, nor do they encourage the growth of normal self-esteem and tolerance of intense affects. Thus her sense of self is tenuous and separates from its archetypal moorings in the Self when her relationship with Hans fails. Elsie is acutely and massively traumatized by his behavior. He becomes a "traumatogenic" object (Balint 1969), repeating her childhood experiences of invalidation and unavailability; her marriage to Hans is a failed *coniunctio* that shatters Elsie's self-structures and the fantasies of connection that hold her together. We see here a failure of love, the real basis of the "glue of the world" that holds us together as selves. We imagine that we are separate, but this is illusory. In fact, we are held together by each other, and enough early, loving experiences of this fact prevent the kind of catastrophe which befalls Elsie.

REFERENCES

Balint, M. 1969. Trauma and object relations. *International Journal of Psychoanalysis* 50: 429–435.
Beebe, B., and Lachmann, F. 1988. Mother-infant influence and precursors of psychic structure. In *Frontiers in Self Psychology: Progress in Self Psychology*, vol. 3., A. Goldberg, ed. Hillsdale, N.J.: The Analytic Press.
Blatt, S. J., and Wild, C. M. 1976. *Schizophrenia: A Developmental Analysis*. New York: Academic Press.
Corbett, L. 1976. Perceptual dyscontrol: A possible organizing principle for schizophrenia research. *Schizophrenia Bulletin* 2(2):249–265.
———. 1989. Kohut and Jung: A comparison of theory and practice. In *Self Psychology, Comparisons and Contrasts*, D. W. Detrick and S. P. Detrick, eds. Hillsdale, N.J.: The Analytic Press.
Edinger, E. F. 1985. *Anatomy of the Psyche*. La Salle, Ill.: Open Court Publishing Company.
Epstein, S., and Coleman, M. 1970. Drive theories of schizophrenias. *Psychosomatic Medicine* 32:113–140.
Jung, C. G. 1944. *Psychology and Alchemy*. CW, vol. 12. Princeton, N.J.: Princeton University Press, 1953.
———. 1948. *Aion: Researches into the Phenomonology of the Self*. CW, vol. 9ii. Princeton, N.J.: Princeton University Press, 1959.
Lidz, T. 1973. *The Origin and Treatment of Schizophrenic Disorders*. New York: Basic Books.
Maier, N. R. F. 1956. Frustration theory: Restatement and extension. *Psychological Review* 63:370–388.

Mednick, S. A. 1958. A learning theory approach to schizophrenia. *Psychological Bulletin* 55:316-327.

Obendorf, C. P. 1941. Time—its relation to reality and purpose. *Psychoanalytic Review* 28:139-155.

Perry, J. W. 1973. *The Self in Psychotic Process.* Dallas: Spring Publications.

Piaget, J. 1969. *The Child's Conception of Time.* A. J. Pomeranz, trans. New York: Basic Books.

Rodnick, E. H. 1973. Antecedents and continuities in schizophreniform behavior. In *Schizophrenia: The First Ten Dean Award Lectures,* S. R. Dean, ed. New York: MSS Information Corporation, pp. 139-161.

Searles, H. F. 1965. *Collected Papers on Schizophrenia and Related Subjects.* New York: International Universities Press.

# "The Girl Without Hands"
# The Redeeming Power of Story

## Daniel A. Lindley

Anyone reading this book is well aware that the reader of fairy tales does not lack for Jungian commentaries on them and the reader of Jung and Jungians does not lack for fairy tales used as amplification and example. For this reason I imagine, at the start, a surfeited reader, eyes slightly glazed over and mind numbed by yet another child lost in the woods or yet another frog prince. Such a reader sinks, in my imagination, into a reverie in which the characters in the stories suddenly appear as players wearing numbered uniforms and there is a program accompanying each story. The program reads: "*27: The King's Mother Complex. 44: The Daughter's Father Complex. 20: The Heroine's Animus. 23: Second Base . . . no, that's wrong, 23 is the Wise Old Woman archetype . . .*" and so on.

Maria Tatar, in a wise and funny book, *The Hard Facts of the Grimms' Fairy Tales* (1987) puts the problem this way:

> That psychoanalytic critics rarely agree on the symbolic meaning of an object or a figure in a tale is . . . not designed to inspire confidence in their methods. When one critic tells us that the dwarves in "Snow White" should be viewed as siblings of the heroine, another asserts that they represent the unconscious, and a third declares them to be symbols of creative activity, is it any wonder that the layman raises an eyebrow in bewilderment? And when we are further offered the option of looking at these figures

as symbolic representations of the heroine's genitals or as a knot of homosexuals, it becomes difficult to stifle a protest. (p. 54)

Indeed it does. To forestall such a protest against what must be seen as yet another Jungian dissection of yet another defenseless tale, I want to put this whole work of reading stories in a larger context. For reading these tales as we try to do is not just an exercise in interpretation. It is an exercise of the symbolic function itself, and that is no small matter.

What I mean is this: many people, probably most people, when they come into analysis, bring with them some particular problem. A painful memory, a relationship gone bad, a work situation no longer satisfying; or, more generally, a feeling that life has lost its savor, its meaning. They ask, as the poet William Wordsworth did in his "Ode: Intimations of Immortality from Recollections of Early Childhood":

> Whither is fled the visionary gleam?
> Where is it now, the glory and the dream?

We start, in the analytic work, with some combination of a feeling-tone and some particulars. The patient feels that the particulars cause the feelings and the feelings then color the particulars. This circularity makes for stuckness, loss of energy, depression, troubles. These feelings and the particulars associated with them make up the content of the early sessions. Often, as Edinger says (1973, p. 40), the patient is surprised to find that the therapist is actually listening.

At some level the patient knows that the analyst knows that the concreteness is part of the problem. The patient is convinced that "there must be more to life than this" (whatever "this" is). But what does the analyst "know"? Actually, probably nothing much more than what the patient knows, if knowledge is defined as the accumulation of experiences. What the analyst has is not knowledge or experience but a way of envisioning knowledge and experience. Essentially, it is what Jung called "the symbolic attitude."

The symbol, Jung said, is that which stands for what is *not yet known*. The symbol embodies life's particulars and transcends them at the same time. For limitless possibility, the sky; for the unconscious, the ocean's depths. For the peace of self-containment, the stone brought back from the shore. For the same peace – but in a dream – a bowl of perfectly still water.

The core of the symbolic attitude is the acceptance of the paradox that we can know and not know, have and not have, at the same moment. We can "have" the symbol – hold the stone, dream the bowl – and yet not ever fully "know" peace. The symbol is an affirmation (and that is why it heals) of possibility. It says, at the same time, "This is" and "This can be."

A character in Djuna Barnes's novel *Nightwood* says, "You have dressed the unknowable in the garments of the known." That is what the symbol does. It is also a way of thinking of Jung's life's work. His entire opus is a description of Jung's own encounters with the "unknowable" psyche. Anima and animus, wise old man and shadow, appeared to Jung as images, as experiences in his life and dreams and in the lives and dreams of his analysands. The patient beginning in analysis often knows only the concrete experiences of an outer life: such people are, to use e. e. cummings's felicitous phrase, "tangled in ropes of thing." But things are invariably only specific bits and pieces of the stream of experience. It is only when they are lifted toward the symbolic that they become beacons rather than entanglements.

Ordinary experience resists being taken symbolically: it insists on its commonness and its "thingness." It is only when we are faced with the new, the unknown, the strange, that the symbolic urge comes upon us. A simple exercise illustrates this. If we draw on a piece of paper a circle, a triangle, and a square and then ask people to name these shapes, they will do so readily. But if we then add a drawing of a free-form enclosed curve, we immediately get metaphors: "Amoeba." "Ink blot." "Blob." "A mess." In the realm of the new and the unknown, metaphor becomes necessary. So it is with symbols: they emerge when we come up against the unknown. And so it is when analysis begins its work of dissolving (ana-*lysis*) thingness. A patient recounts an anecdote about slamming a door. The analyst inquires on which side of the door the patient ended up; it turns out that the patient was now in a room with no other way out. "Do you want to be in a place where the only way out is through the same place you have just tried to shut yourself out of?" asks the analyst. "Not really." "Have you ever done that before? Trapped yourself that way?" And the patient reflects, and begins to sense other instances. The door is becoming a symbol. The patient is beginning to develop the symbolic attitude, the attitude that will say, finally, that things, experiences, life itself, have meaning – and, ultimately, therefore, value. This is what "The Girl Without Hands" is about.

I propose now to take you through the basic plot of the story and then to amplify elements of that plot. You must decide for yourself which amplifications make sense to you and which seem far-fetched. Throughout, though, I hope you will bear in mind the idea of the symbolic attitude and its healing potential. If we stay literal with the story we will be no more moved along than is a patient who still feels caught in the nitty-gritties of daily living; and if we jump too quickly into a Jungian (or any other) symbol system, we will have merely created a new mystery, leaving us, as Anna Russell said, "as befogged as before." I am trying for a middle ground between literal mud and symbolic airheadedness. That done, I shall return to the theme of the symbolic attitude.

## The Girl Without Hands

Once upon a time there was a certain miller who had fallen bit by bit into poverty until he had nothing left but his mill and an old apple tree which grew behind it. One day when he had gone into the forest to cut wood, an old man whom he had never seen before stepped up to him and promised the miller enormous wealth in return for "what is standing behind your old mill." The miller, thinking the stranger must mean only the old apple tree, agreed. The stranger, however, laughed ominously and said: "Remember, in three years' time I will come to your mill and carry away what belongs to me."

When the miller got home, his wife came running out to meet him. She called out, "Tell me, miller, whatever happened while you were gone? We have become rich. No one came here, and I can't imagine how this has happened." The miller then explained what had happened and how he had given up (as he thought) the old apple tree. But his wife was horrified because, as she told him, it was actually their daughter who was standing behind the mill, sweeping the yard. Since it was the daughter whom the old man wanted, the old man must be the devil himself.

Their daughter, a beautiful and devout girl, lived through the three years without blame. On the day the devil came for her she washed herself clean and drew a chalk circle around herself. These acts prevented the devil from approaching her. The devil demanded that the miller take the water away from her so he could approach her, but she wept on her hands and so kept them pure. The devil next demanded that the miller chop off his daughter's hands. The miller was shocked, but the devil told him that either he did what he was told or it would be the miller himself whom the devil would carry off. The miller, terrified, told his daughter what he must do and asked for her forgiveness. She replied that, because she was his daughter, he could do whatever he needed to do to her. And she put down both her hands and let him chop them off. The devil then came for her a third time, but the daughter had wept so much on her maimed arms that they were washed clean with her tears. At this the devil had to give in.

Then the miller said to his daughter that, since it was through her sacrifice that they have received great wealth, he would keep her "handsomely" as long as she lived. But the girl replied that she could not stay. She must go out into the larger world. She asked that her arms be tied behind her, and she said that compassionate people would take care of her. And, at sunrise, she left her home.

The daughter (now referred to as "the maiden") walked all day and grew hungry. She spied a "royal garden" with a beautiful fruit-laden pear tree in it and prayed to God. An angel then appeared and parted the water in the moat that surrounded the garden. The maiden ate one of the pears by biting it off the tree with her mouth. The king's gardener saw all this. The next morning when the king counted his pears, he found that one was missing. The gardener and the king kept watched the next night and, together with a priest, saw the angel and the maiden appear again. This time the priest asked the maiden whether she was a spirit or a mortal, and she explained that she was "an unhappy mortal deserted by all but the grace of God." The king replied that even though she had been forsaken by all the world, he would not forsake her. He took her to his palace, fell in love with her, married her, and had a pair of silver hands made for her.

After a year the king had to go on a journey, so he gave his young queen over to the care of his mother and told her to write at once should the queen give birth to a child and to take care of both until his return. The queen indeed gave birth to a fine baby boy. There now followed a whole sequence of letters sent and inter-cepted, of messengers who fell asleep — with various disastrous results. The devil substituted a letter to the king saying the child was a monster; next, he substituted a return letter in which the king ordered his mother to kill the queen and the monster; the mother was horrified and instead sent the queen and her child off into "a wild and deep wood" where the queen once again prayed and was once again saved and watched over by an angel, for seven years. During that time, by God's grace, her true hands grew back.

When the king returned from his journey, he naturally wanted to see his child and his queen. His mother showed him the letters the devil had forged commanding that the queen and her child be killed, and she explained how she sent them off into the woods instead. The king searched for them for seven years. Finally, he found them; but he did not recognize them, especially because his queen now had her own hands again. But the angel produced the silver hands from the back of the little house in which they had been living and then he knew. They returned home to the palace and to the king's old mother. Everyone rejoiced; the king and queen were married once again and lived "contentedly to their happy end."

## INTERPRETATION

Now let us review what has happened in this story. To begin with, we have the miller's slow descent into poverty. We do not know what brought the miller to this point in his life, but we know that he *was* a miller, a person with a role in the community, but now the mill no longer feeds him. What he thought he was has come to an end; his persona is dissolving. This makes him dangerous at home. How often have we heard, "Everything was fine until the store failed. Then he started to drink . . ." or some such account. But for now he still has his mill (his old workplace) and an apple tree, representing the possibility of choice between good and evil.

Next we have the offer of riches from the strange old man. This is, for the miller, the Easy Way Out: the miller will have his problems solved without doing anything. It is an "outside" solution (like gambling or alcohol), avoiding any inward journey. The miller thinks not of his daughter but of the apple tree. If this is what the miller must give up, then the "old man" will possess the apple tree, the symbol, again, of choice, of free will. Of course, this is not what the old man is after; the old man already understands the principle of choice, since he has offered one. But the miller does not feel he has made a choice; he thinks he has changed his life from one of poverty to one of prosperity by giving up an apple tree. He would say he "had no choice," by way of excuse; but giving up the apple tree is far more important than the miller realizes. Make a pact with the devil and you give up free choice. The miller would have been well-advised to think long and hard about what an apple tree represents instead of giving it up so easily.

When he returns home, his wife, in spite of her fantastic news about the new wealth, addresses him as "miller." This is a small point but an important one. She sees him not as husband, or father, or even a whole person, but only as he has seen himself: only as "miller," in his social role. And this is the first mention of a wife. The miller, conversing with the old man, has not thought of her at all. He thinks only of his own situation and his own problems. Such a husband is problem enough, and of course we shall soon see him equally self-centered as a father.

There is one thing to be said for his wife. She has enough sense to be puzzled. If she were merely celebrating she would be caught in the same folly as her husband is. There is a split in this marriage: the husband lives in the world of appearances, of keeping up a front, while the wife seeks deeper causes. It is she, therefore, who tells the miller that it was their daughter he has actually given up.

The daughter lives the three years without blame. She is, at this point, a "good girl" in the confining sense of being dutiful. But being dutiful can have horrifying consequences for the soul. In the amputation scene we see with terrifying clarity the whole dynamic of the father who abuses his daughter. The father thinks only of himself. Theoretically the daughter has to choose between defying him and submitting to him, but there really is no choice, because to defy is to risk abandonment and death. This is the daughter who goes along with everything because to do otherwise results in the father's rage, in his staying away from home, in his drinking, in a thousand acts of abandonment that make the abuse seem the lesser threat. "I do this because this is how I love you," says the abusing father, and the daughter feels, "Better I let him love me in this way than that he leave us because I refuse him." Unconsciously the daughter has taken on the role of mother and wife: she is keeping the family together by submitting to father's demands. She gives up her hands – her possibility of acting for herself in the world – in order to preserve the only security she knows. Many people wonder why children stay in an abusive relationship, sometimes for years. The common threat, "I'll kill you if you tell," is translated by the child into a deeper fear: that father will abandon the whole family if she does not do his bidding. And this abandonment means certain death for everyone except father. The daughter manages to keep the devil at bay with her rituals involving wholeness (the circle) and purity (the water). Indeed the devil, we are told, has lost all right over her. (Of course this turns out not to be true – the false letters are to come.) Keeping the devil at bay with her tears and her circle-drawing is a victory of a sort. But she has not kept her own father at bay. To put it another way, she has not kept the devil-in-her-father at bay. He is still in control of everything. It is this control which the daughter must now proceed to undo, for her own individuation's sake. We will see how he tries to maintain his control and what she does about it.

Now the father offers to keep his daughter handsomely all her life. Note this carefully: he offers to *keep* her. There will be no life for her on her own. This father cannot let go of the only way of life he knows. He is completely dependent on having power over his daughter.

I have had in my own practice a daughter who had such a father. All during her growing up she was in thrall to him in just the way that our story portrays. But after graduation from her parochial high school, she entered a convent. In this way she solved, in one move, two problems: leaving home and cutting off any further threat from the possible sexualization of her relationship with her father. I shall return to her at a later point in our story. For now, note that the daughter in the tale knows that she must leave even though she is without hands. The system of dependency at home meets her father's needs but not hers, and the daughter's need to individuate turns out to be a wondrously positive force. It takes courage – and faith. She has both.

Now we come to the king's garden and the angel. The angel changes the rules by which the natural world, the world of things, works. By praying, the maiden has invoked what Jung called the transcendent function, the link between ordinary experience and the symbolic. I will return to this idea after the explication of our tale. Incidentally, a king who counts his pears every day apparently has an obsessive-compulsive streak!

In any event, stealing fruit from the forbidden garden does some good after all – as we know from Genesis.

So the king takes up the maiden, and they marry. Why isn't this the end of our story: "And the king and queen lived happily ever after"? After all, she has been saved; why shouldn't they?

Because her silver hands are the king's creation, that's why. True, she has escaped her father's narrow and punitive world, but she has now become the king's creature, with *his* hands. Gertrud

Mueller Nelson, discussing this tale in *Here All Dwell Free*, compares the queen's role with that of the corporate wife who advances her husband's career and does his bidding. Our heroine is now well off, but she is her husband's adjunct, no more. How often, in American political life, do we see wives with such silver hands? Is the American public ready for wives with hands of their own? This is the issue, in a popular-magazine sense, at this point in the story. More deeply, it is a feminist issue of genuine significance.

Now the king has to go on a journey of his own. The world does not stand still, even for happiness. The king has some growing up to do too, so his bride is left in the care of her mother-in-law. The king's idea of mothering is carried by his actual mother, not the mother of his child-to-be; or, if you prefer, it is his mother complex, more than the actual mother, who will inhabit the nursery. Hardly fertile ground for our young queen to grow in.

Then there is the series of incidents around messengers and letters. A messenger falls asleep; this sleep allows the old father-evil to appear again – the old, destructive, murderous, abandoning father. A good messenger, a conscientious messenger, bridges the distance between conscious and unconscious, between the literal and the symbolic. (Hermes, the good messenger, doesn't sleep. That, by the way, is the difference between myth and fairy tale. The gods and goddesses of myth are *constants*, always acting in the same way, and so represent archetypes. The characters in fairy tales are idiosyncratic victims, acting out pathology, or they are idiosyncratic heroes or heroines, acting out transformations and individuations.)

The queen wanders in the wood. Obviously she has to be away from the palace, the "only-queen" role, to find herself in the wood. My patient, the one I mentioned above, came into analysis at essentially this point. A major task has been for her to "grow back" her hands. A major task for me has been to *not* be the king-in-the-palace in the transference. If our work is to succeed at all, I too have to be seen by her – and see myself – as "on a journey." It is valuable when my patient and I see each other as searching in the wood that we share. Each of us was threatened, and we were both put out in the world to fend for ourselves, albeit in very different ways and under different circumstances.

Finally, the king finds his queen, and the child, and they are married once again, with great ceremony. Of the final marriage we can say that it symbolizes that they are now both complete.

*Now*, and only now, can they live out the rest of their lives in an equal, and fulfilling, relationship.

Imagine again for a moment that jaded reader I postulated at the start. Such a reader might well be thinking, "That's how fairy tales end: 'They lived happily ever after.' Don't they always?" But that circumstance, happy as it is, is not the point. The real point is the leaving of home. The heroine of our story will come to see, after she leaves, that individuation is a process that happens naturally and therefore one in which she can, perhaps must, take part. And see this in spite of the very real difficulties that have been thrown in her path.

This is true in analysis and in ordinary life as well. In order to insist upon individuation as the real point of this story, I will provide another, contemporary version. Here, from the *Chicago Tribune* (7 June 1992) is a bit of a profile of an actress, Dana Delany:

> [Her] family was comfortable. Her father owned a company that manufactured toilet flush valves. But the family was not without its problems.
>
> "From the outside, we were the typical American family—schools, vacations, church, those things," says Dana Delany. [Here is the miller's persona, in modern form.] "Of course, underneath we had the usual family problems nobody ever talked about. . . ."
>
> "I wanted people to like me, to accept me," she says. "I was very much concerned with being a girlfriend, having a boyfriend (she and actor Treat Williams were together for four years). It was not until I was nearly 30 that I started doing things for myself."
>
> The breakup of her relationship with Williams—his choice—was catalytic.
>
> "It kind of kicked me out of the house, metaphorically, though I didn't know it at the time," she says. "I was devastated, but it was the best thing that could have happened to me."
>
> She went to Los Angeles to act. . . . Supporting movie and television roles began coming her way, one after another.

It is very much worth noting that Ms. Delany is able to see the *metaphor* of being "kicked out of the house." She has moved on her own toward a symbolic attitude. It is this, I would argue, that had to happen before she could begin to "do things for herself." And it was not until she started to do things for herself—that is, with her own hands—that her life began to have form and purpose. And *that* is the point.

To recapitulate, then, "The Girl Without Hands": the story starts in perfect literalness – a miller has fallen on hard times. To alleviate this he makes a pact with the devil that draws his innocent daughter into grave danger and ultimately a terrible mutilation, the amputation of her hands. Here is a father who must preserve his power at all costs, literally. Seen literally, he is pathologically self-centered, knowing only himself, narcissistic to the point where we do not even hear of his wife and daughter until we have visited the self-centered depths of his one-sided psyche. People so narcissistic are most difficult acquaintances and most dreadful parents: friends and children are shunted aside, ignored, *used*. The devil brings the first symbol to this story. If we say a person is "possessed" by the devil, though, immediately we define the problem as one not caused by a fault in the person but by the one-sidedness of the devil. The devil is the devil because he acts only in his own self-interest. His self-interest is his entire being, and we *know* that this is evil. The devil puts the illness "out there" where we can see it. A patient will say that her abusive father "couldn't help it," or "that's the way he was." An aura of helplessness clouds this history. But the devil we can see. We are thus helped by the clarity of the symbol as compared with the dark, unpredictable, relentless intractability of a cruel father in daily experience.

Then along comes the king. Offering, as he does, love, security, and silver hands, he offers a life, of a sort. We see security and status in the collective personified. Once again the symbol clarifies. But there is another side: "After a year, the king had to go on a journey." With kingship comes responsibility. A king is not so much master as servant, to duty and the "real world." And because this is the one world he knows, he *assumes* his wife wants to be in the same world. His real problem is that he knows no other. But when he returns to find his wife and child gone, the importance of his public duty pales and he sets out (at last) on a true quest. My patient came into analysis to grow back her true hands. This king might well come at this moment of loss, to find a helper in the quest he must undertake. For him the metaphor of analysis as an *assisted journey* would be apt indeed.

Finally, once again, to the symbolic attitude. This story above all describes the individuation of its heroine. For this to occur the story must unfold in the way it does. There must be a miller, to represent the literal world and the world of the persona, but he must fall on hard times, to show that the outer world is insufficiently nourishing; there must be a devil, or else the story (as a story of the daughter's life) would never get underway. That is to say, a daughter who stays in thrall to her father cannot begin her own life. Also, the shadow (of the father—his possessiveness) with its one-sidedness is necessary, and is represented by the devil. There must be a king (to represent the good life of the collective) but this good life is not sufficient in itself. Above all these there must be an innocent, dutiful daughter who must grow up; and she would never have grown unless she had had to leave home, thus initiating her individuation by enacting the symbol of the heroine's acceptance of the call to adventure, the call also to a higher level of meaning. Note "enacting the symbol." In this phrase the transcendent function, the bridging of world and image, is reflected. Finally, above her are the angels, representing the magical connection between daily life and the implicate order that showers its grace down, but only when we are open to it. The story unfolds and our awareness grows. Story, like the transcendent function, links the literal with the symbolic by posing a series of situations that lead, one after another, to a final internalization of the symbolic attitude *in us*. To know what "hands" are— the capacity to shape one's own life—this heroine had to first lose her hands, then have silver ones, before she grew into her true nature. *Her story causes awareness—hers and ours—*through its portrayal of hands as symbol. The hands are first in the service only of father, then only in the service of king; finally, they are her own. It is only when we have learned to use our own hands in ways that are true to our own nature that we may say we are fully, responsibly in the world. This the story shows us by encouraging us—no, really requiring us—to leave the literal and enter the symbolic world where, when the story ends, the true hands of the true queen are her strength, her power—no less real than those of the king and really more valuable for having been earned. And no less real than ours, if we have traveled this road. The traveling of the road is a narrative, a story. It is story that moves us along.

For me the great master of story is Prospero, in Shakespeare's *The Tempest*. His enemies are shipwrecked on his island in various states of psychic disrepair. Gradually, through his magic and his magical, angellike messenger, Ariel, Prospero shapes and reshapes their psyches through the artifice of a magical pageant (not unlike a fairy tale) until, finally, he can achieve the blowing away of "the ignorant fumes that mantle their purer reason," and they can see the world as it is because they have experienced the story, the visions and encounters on the island that he has produced for them. Through the same means he brings his daughter Miranda to consciousness and to love. Here is how he explains what he has done:

> Our revels now are ended. These our actors,
> As I foretold you, were all spirits, and
> Are melted into air, into thin air:
> And, like the baseless fabric of this vision,
> The cloud-capp'd towers, the gorgeous palaces,
> The solemn temples, the great globe itself,
> Yea, all which it inherit, shall dissolve,
> And, like this insubstantial pageant faded,
> Leave not a rack behind. We are such stuff
> As dreams are made on; and our little life
> Is rounded with a sleep.

This Prospero tells them, but only when they are ready, finally, to hear. They have not only seen the symbols, as we do when we read these tales. They are on their way to living symbolically, too. The experience of story, perhaps especially of the unexpected stories that fairy tales are, pushes us toward the symbolic attitude, for without it the stories remain simply strange, as do our dreams, if too quickly forgotten. But both fairy tales and dreams have an eerie clarity; thus they compel our attention.

We are indeed such stuff as dreams are made on. Our dreams are stories too. They lift us away from the literal and into the realm of once upon a time, the realm "where wishing once worked" – and, if we are open to it, still does. The chasm between daily, ordinary life and the ineffable realm of archetype, pure form, symbol – this chasm is bridged by story and by dream. The telling of "The Girl Without Hands" moves us along by reminding us that it is our hands that make it possible for us to act in the world. But they must be *our* hands, not the king's. Furthermore the cruelest father cannot sever them from us once we choose to go on the journey. But we must choose. In a house newly filled with wealth, the wounded daughter speaks: "Here I cannot stay." In that moment her redemption is assured, because in that moment her story begins.

## REFERENCES

Barnes, D. 1937. *Nightwood*. New York: Harcourt, Brace.
Edinger, E. 1973. *Ego and Archetype*. New York: Penguin Books.
Jung, C. G. 1921. *Psychological Types*. *CW*, vol. 6. Princeton, N.J.:
    Princeton University Press, 1971.
Nelson, G. M. 1991. *Here All Dwell Free*. New York: Doubleday.
Tatar, M. 1987. *The Hard Facts of the Grimms' Fairy Tales*. Princeton,
    N.J.: Princeton University Press.

# "Snow White"
# Desire, Death, and Transformation

## Nancy Dougherty

Fairy tales express eternal patterns that weave threads between cultures and stitch together history. Being made of symbolic stuff, multivalent interpretive perspectives are possible. I will explore the themes of desire, death, and transformation in Snow White with three complementary perspectives in mind: analytically, as an archetypal pattern in a woman's individuation[1]; psychologically, as a problem of the regressed ego or the "true self" (Winnicott 1960); and theologically, as a meeting of one's soul through the vehicle of desire. We can imagine the heroine of this tale as referring to either the development of a woman's sense of self or the development of a man's anima.

The story of Snow White particularly brings to light how the path to the sleeping soul is forged by the energy of desire. In the

---

[1] According to a 1987 lecture by Jungian analyst Beverly Zabriskie, the following are some common mythic themes in feminine individuation:

1. Disobedience required to separate from her family of origin. She must leave the original container to become her own container.
2. She leaves to connect with the other, using the family's magic or secrets to help the hero/rescuer.
3. She merges with the other.
4. A loss, betrayal, abandonment, expulsion, or dismemberment of or from the other occurs.
5. Suffering leads to wisdom and love. Or she refuses to suffer, which leads to bitterness and love magic.

risky process of reaching out and moving toward what she desires, Snow White illuminates the process of soul-making. Here the relationship between desire and connecting to one's true heart is expressed.

Reaching toward our desires can lead us into either fuller participation in life and its bounty or into empty states of loss. Frustrated desire can evoke painful longing, ego death, and the possibility of transformation. These experiences of failure and despair can be signposts on the road to creating a personal sense of soul and meaning in one's life. The motif of the sleeping soul is an ancient one. In the following paragraph, author P. L. Travers (1975) amplifies this dynamic:

> Are we dealing here with the sleeping soul and all the external affairs of life that hem it in and hide it; something that falls asleep after childhood, something that, not to waken, would make life meaningless? One thing is certain. The sleeper is not merely a pretty girl waiting, after an eon of dreams, to be awakened by a lover. She is a symbol, the core and heart of the world she inhabits.

## Snow White

O nce there was a queen who wished for a daughter who would be a beautiful reflection of herself. However, the moment the infant princess Snow White was born, the queen died. One year later, Snow White's father, the king, took a new bride. The new queen was haughty and vain, but also a woman of considerable magic.

When Snow White turned seven, her stepmother consulted her magic mirror and discovered that she was no longer the most beautiful female in the kingdom. Upon hearing this, the new queen turned yellow and green with envy and ordered a hunter to kill the child. However, out of pity, he turned Snow White free into the woods alone.

Snow White found her way through the woods to the tidy home of the seven dwarfs. After some initial negotiation, they welcomed her as a sort of housekeeper/mother figure. Meanwhile, back at the palace, the magic mirror informed the queen that Snow White still lived. Now the queen became more determined than ever to kill the child, as her envy gave her no rest. The queen made three murder attempts upon the child, each one more successful than the last.

In three different visits, disguised as a peddler, the wicked queen tempted Snow White into accepting a comb, stay laces for her waist, and a poison apple. Snow White passed out after receiving the first two gifts, but the dwarfs arrived home in time to revive her. Eating the poison apple seemed to be fatal. Unable to arouse Snow White, the Seven Dwarfs placed her in a glass coffin and mourned her demise. Over time, the coffin was visited by an owl, a raven, and a dove.

Riding through the woods one day, a prince from another kingdom saw the princess in the glass coffin and fell in love with her. The prince ordered his men to remove the coffin, and in doing so, the piece of apple stuck in her throat was dislodged. Snow White then awoke and fell in love with the prince. A wedding celebration was planned. The wicked stepmother was invited to the reception, where she was forced to dance to her death in red hot iron shoes.

## INTERPRETATION

This tale opens, "Once upon a time in the middle of winter when the flakes of snow were falling like feathers from the sky" (all of the following quotes are taken from Grimm 1944). It begins in the timelessness of the unconscious, in the season of death. Feathers are images of air, wind, speed, and height. They fall from the sky, the realm of the spirit, covering earth in icy stillness. Winter is the season when Persephone dwells in the Underworld with Hades, leaving Demeter above awaiting her return. The ruling feminine principle is in a melancholy, unfulfilled state, separated from the earth by a layer of cold snow. Yet winter is also the season that precedes the annual renewal of spring.

> When a woman is the chief character in a story, it is a sign of the theme's antiquity. It takes us back to those cloudy eras when the world was ruled, not by a god, as it was in later years, but by the Great Goddess. (Travers 1975, p. 59)

The queen wishes for a child who is "white as snow, red as blood, and black as ebony." Red, white, and black are colors sacred to the Great Goddess (Walker 1983). These colors represent Her symbolic threefold nature: spring, summer, and winter; the maiden, the mother, and the crone; Snow White, Demeter, and Hecate. The wholeness inherent in the divine feminine trinity is embodied within the structure of this story. Snow White leaves maidenhood when she reaches out for womanly fullness. This is presented in the symbolic form of the apple of life, offered to her by the crone. Through her death to maidenhood, she is able to awaken to her own potential to become a queen. "The neophyte dies – or sleeps – on one level and awakes on another, as chrysalis wakes into butterfly" (Travers 1975, p. 60).

The queen wishes for a child born in the mirror image of her current experience, introducing the theme of narcissism to the tale. Perhaps in an attempt to overcome her melancholy, Snow White's mother hopes to find her life's meaning through her child. Sewing is a meditative/reflective task, and it's while sewing that the queen is wounded. I imagine she does not suffer the pain of her wound but escapes into the fantasy of desiring a child to mirror her and carry her feminine suffering for her.

The tricolor initial image informs us of the child's potential to experience and embody all three aspects of the archetypal feminine. However, Snow White is named only for the color which symbolically represents purity, chastity, and innocence. These are the qualities most preferred by Western culture in its girls and princesses. Yet existent *in potentia* in the image of snow is the water of life. Thus the heroine is endowed at birth with the *prima materia* needed for her own transformation.

However, if one lingers too long in childhood, white can also be the color of coldness, impotence, and frigidity.[2] Snow White is named for the spiritual realm of upper air, not for earth and sexuality nor death and the underworld. These other qualities she will have to connect with on her own. They are offered to her by the wicked stepmother, the Dark Goddess that her mother never came to know. Symbolically integrating the red and the black represents the initiation issues that confront a woman who seeks to move from living life as a girl to the possibility of living life as an adult woman.

The Grimms' version of "Little Snow White" does not open with another royal couple wishing for an heir to the throne but with a queen hoping for a daughter. Soon after she receives her wish, the queen dies. This story also tells about the multiple problems of being unmothered. Without adequate maternal mirroring and guidance, children cannot feel valued for being themselves and therefore cannot develop sound boundaries or learn to

---

[2]I find it interesting that Ad deVries identifies white as "the favorite color of narcissistic women" (p. 499).

make good choices. In such a state, one can become vulnerable to living an unconscious life of serving others, and one is open to being easily invaded. In such a state, a child's experience of being is interrupted and eclipsed too early by a defensive identification with doing. A helpful "false self" adaptation may enable survival while simultaneously inhibiting a rich, full life grounded in a living connection to the Self.

To meet her "true self," Snow White must be tempted, act on her own desire, and suffer the subsequent consequences. In this transformative process, she deepens her positive relationship with nature by reconnecting with her own instincts. At one with nature and following the heart's desire, one's heart and elemental soul increase in synchrony.

"And when the child was born, the Queen died. After one year had passed, the King took himself another wife." Psychologically speaking, living without a mother in the first year of her life, Snow White missed the essential mirroring process and bonding with a "good enough" mother that a child needs to forge a connection with her "true self." Where girl children are not valued equally with boys, it is all too common that unmothered women beget unmothered daughters. These mothers may seek to fill the void in their own mirroring process by expecting their children to do it for them. In a childhood sacrificed to meeting a parent's needs, the child loses the possibility of developing a living connection to the Self (Miller 1981). This tragic reenactment is poetically expressed by Anne Sexton (1960):

> I, who was never quite sure
> about being a girl, needed another
> life, another image to remind me.
>
> And this was my worst guilt; you could not cure
> nor soothe it. I made you to find me.

A shallow identity based on external adaptation rather than a living inner connection to the Self casts a very dark shadow. As innocent Snow White is born and named, the "false bride" is constellated in the unconscious. This is the shadow side of the queen. The false bride and its relationship to narcissism is detailed by Jungian analyst Nathan Schwartz-Salant (1982):

> The false bride represents a wrong connection to the Self in terms of concern with power, and it manifests in the identification with

appearance. Just as the witch in Snow White has a magic mirror that she consults to assure herself of her beauty over all others, so too the bewitched feminine side of the narcissistic character (whether male or female), rather than relating the ego to the Self, turns psychic energy back onto the ego. Hence the person is always referring internal and external events to his or her own ego. (p. 40)

The erection of a false self defense makes a secure ego/Self connection impossible. With a good enough ego/Self connection, there is a flow of authentic desire or libido that is both a grounding internal connection and a dynamic guide into the world. The careful, conscious following of our authentic desire can lead us into a developed life of meaning and creativity. The false self defense prevents an embodied experience of living identity. What remains for the narcissistic personality is a cold and empty inner world, often full of crushing demands.

Though Snow White's father is alive, no further mention is made of him in the tale. This absent father abandons his daughter to his "proud and haughty" second wife. The stepmother, now acting out the role of the false bride, demands constant positive mirroring and becomes ruthless when she does not receive it. This dark queen frequently consults the magic mirror about her beauty. Her driven quest for positive mirroring illustrates how the suffering that could lead to meaning and connection is prevented.

Seven years later, one full cycle, the queen's mirror proclaims Snow White more beautiful than she. The queen turns yellow and green with envy. Rage pours through her injured pride, and her beautiful facade shatters as she orders the huntsman to kill Snow White in the forest. As envy erupts, the dark queen's adaptation is overwhelmed by her unintegrated dark side. And while yellow and green are the colors of *putrefactio* and envy, they are also the color of the sun and new growth. Paradoxically, as the terrible mother condemns Snow White to death, she moves the child along toward adulthood.

In this tale, as in many others, it is the shadow that forces or entices the heroine to do the one thing that will lead her to consciousness.

Only the integration of good and evil and the stern acceptance of the opposites will change the situation and bring about the condition that is known as "Happy Ever After." Without the

Wicked Fairy Godmother or Evil Stepmother, there would be no story. She, not the heroine, is the Goddess in the machine. The true mother, by her very nature, is bound to protect and comfort; this is why she is so often disposed of before the story begins. . . . It is the stepmother, her cold heart unwillingly cooperating with the heroine's need, who thrusts the child from the warm hearth, out from the sheltering walls of home to find her own true way. (Travers 1975, p. 57)

The huntsman is a father figure just as the wicked queen is a mother figure. He acts "as if" he obeys the queen's command to kill Snow White yet spares the child's life at the last moment. And while this enables her to escape into the darkness of the forest, this has always seemed to me a paltry act of mercy. He abandons her to the forest with the assumption that she will be devoured by wild beasts. He is not conscious of the possibility of a different connection to nature and the instincts. The queen has ordered the huntsman to bring her Snow White's lungs and liver as a token of the deed done. The huntsman brings back those of a boar, an animal sacred to the Great Goddess Herself.

The wicked queen had the cook roast and salt these, and then she ate them. The lungs facilitate the movement of the breath, pneuma, spirit. And the liver was thought to be the seat of the soul by the ancients. Thus, the queen wished to incorporate the spirit and soul she did not have access to on her own. Thinking she had eaten Snow White makes the queen the ultimate devouring mother!

Snow White is representative of the positive, life-asserting qualities that threaten the insecure, narcissistic personality. When the wicked stepmother devours what she believes to be Snow White's vital organs, she recaptures a primitive cannibalistic expression of envy: the belief that one acquires the power and characteristics of what one eats. (Kolbenschlag 1979, p. 31)

It is when Snow White turns seven that she is forced into the woods. Seven is a number of completion of a cycle, of the endless round, as in the seven planets or seven days of the week. It is at age seven that Christian children make their first communion. I remember when I was that age being told that at seven children are able to distinguish between right and wrong and therefore are capable of sin, thus making the sacraments of confession and communion timely. At this time of budding consciousness and responsibility, Snow White is alone and on her own. Contrary to the huntsman's expectations, she goes undisturbed by the beasts of the realm. Without a relationship that could have helped her develop a more conscious sense of feminine identity, Snow White descends deeper into the unconscious realm. In the darkness of these woods she is not only able to survive but is in a place where she can begin to develop a living connection to the Self.

"She ran as long as her feet would go until it was almost evening," the story tells us. Then Snow White comes upon the home of the seven dwarfs which was "neater and cleaner than can be told." The cottage and its contents have been left in obsessive order. All the tables and beds are covered with white cloth. Though she is hungry, Snow White eats from each place in moderation and says her prayers before going to sleep. This is early evidence that she has a good potential for mature relating. She has a capacity to consider the needs of others, and her prayers show acknowledgment of a power greater than she.

These dwarfs, unlike the fellows in the Disney version, are all alike, not differentiated from each other. In terms of the masculine they are hardly differentiated at all. Dwarfs are said to have no parents and do not marry or have children. Bettleheim observes that the dwarfs "fail to develop into mature humanity, are permanently arrested on a pre-oedipal level" (1977, p. 200). We could say their development is parallel to Snow White's undifferentiated state at this point in the story. Snow White's childlike feminine psyche can only relate to the dwarfed masculine:

> Dwarfs are hard-working and clever at their trade. Work is the essence of their lives; they know nothing of leisure and recreation. Although they are impressed by her beauty and moved by her tale of misfortune, they make it clear right away that the price of living with them is engaging in conscientious work. (Kolbenschlag 1979, p. 209)

The seven dwarfs say to Snow White, "If you will take care of our house, cook, make the beds, wash, sew, and knit, and if you will keep everything neat and clean, you can stay with us and you shall want for nothing." Evidently love, sex, and the pleasures and challenges of relationship all are beyond the capacity of the dwarfs' imagination. I was interested that the tale has them mining for copper and gold, in that order. While gold is symbolic of the completed work of individuation, copper is the metal of

Venus. Perhaps it is necessary for them to mine (unearth, connect with) copper in order to get to the gold, that is, make a proper connection to love and relatedness to become whole. Their assumption that Snow White will "want for nothing" reflects their lack of awareness of a young woman's needs. They seem to have no concept of Snow White as an individual with a path of her own to follow.

They do warn her not to let the stepmother in, but are unable to help her relate to womanhood in a more mature way.

> The dwarfs are fixed in their development; in contrast to Snow White, their lives are conflict-free, they are excluded from the process of transformation. Help for Snow White must come from beyond. (Kolbenschlag 1979, p. 32)

Why is Snow White unable to make use of their warnings and concern for her safety? What does the queen offer her that's more tempting than the tidy and conflict-free life she lives in the home of the Seven Dwarfs? Like her mythic sisters, Psyche peeking at the beauty ointment and Persephone reaching out for the beauty she saw in the narcissus flower, Snow White is tempted and falls through the force of her own desire. She needs to develop a living relationship to the feminine, which is beyond the world of the dwarfs. Because she is living a life that is too small and sterile for her developing nature, the dark queen is able to tempt her with symbols of a fuller life beyond the neat cottage. The first temptation Snow White succumbs to is the multicolored stay laces offered to her by the disguised queen. I imagine these laces gaily define her developing feminine figure as she grows from childhood to adolescence. A new power is growing within her. Here, innocent Snow White receives the wicked stepmother disguised as an old peddler woman, without any discrimination. The queen entices her with the vaguely parental and guilt-invoking line, "What a fright you look. Come, I will lace you properly for once!" She pulls the laces tighter and tighter until Snow White faints for lack of air.

The dwarfs come home and revive her by undoing the laces and warn her again not to allow anyone in when she is alone. Again the mirror informs the queen of Snow White's life and beauty. This time the queen turns to witchcraft to concoct a poisonous comb – thus confirming, if any of us still had a doubt, that the wicked queen is indeed a true witch. Only mildly more cautious and discriminating, this time Snow White lets herself be beguiled.

The comb is a symbol for fertility and rain, also vanity and restlessness (deVries 1974). I imagine Snow White putting up her hair (sexuality, energy, primitive instinct) with a comb in the way that many young girls experiment with their attractiveness. Thus she succumbs a second time to flirting with the world outside of her narrow life with the dwarfs. The stirrings of womanhood beckon.

"Now I will comb you properly for once," says the queen, and with those words she does her deed. And again, the dwarfs revive Snow White and issue their warning. The third time the mirror informs her of Snow White's life and beauty, the queen exhibits a cold, narcissistic rage and an envy so great that she would trade her life for revenge. "Snow White shall die, even if it costs me my life!" she cries. This is one of the darkest moments in the story. In terms of psychological development, there can be a corollary moment in analysis when deeply hidden destructive urges emerge. While rage that is unconsciously maintained creates a certain intrapsychic stasis, unleashed it creates a disintegration through which a more stable connection to the Self can be forged. Returning to Schwartz-Salant's (1982) analysis:

> Envy is the dark side of the narcissistic character. I view it with a great importance, because I find it to be the "psychic glue," the element of affinity that keeps the components of the self (small 's' self), in its grandiose form, cohesively together. Dealing with envy, and its associated components of rage and sadism, can allow the deintegration of this self structure. As a result, a properly functioning anima or animus can emerge. (p. 42)

It is in her moment of rage that the queen creates Snow White's third temptation, the death apple. She used her magic so that only one half of it was poisoned. Snow White longed to taste the apple, and when she saw that the woman ate part of it, she could resist no longer, stretched out her hand, and took the poisonous half. No sooner had she bitten into it than she fell dead. From her longing, she has reached out for the object of her desire. She has eaten the red portion (life, blood, eroticism), which initiates her into the experience of the blackness of death. Snow White has now experienced the triune color symbolism of the Great Goddess.

Like her sisters in myth, Persephone and Psyche, Snow White acts on her desire. She is no longer the child residing in the world of obedient safety but rather a young woman moved to action by her own longings. She reaches out past her approval-seeking adaptations into the mysteries that only her own desire can reveal to her. Her reaching out, and the resultant fall and descent, take her to the unique place where a deep reconnection can occur.

> Persephone isn't just playing about when she is raped: she is reaching for something ecstatic, transcendent. There is a proper way to enter Hades, the realm of death, a way of transformation. Falling into it, for example, in depression, narcissistic injury, psychosis, etc., is not necessarily a way of transformation. Often one just comes back with nothing changed. But there is a way set out, and it involves reaching for the excess of Dionysian spirit, for joy. (Schwartz-Salant 1982, p. 144)

The apple represents totality, earthly material desires, summer's maturity, and sexual enjoyment. Apples are known as the fruit of Venus. They are also the fruit of autumn.

> As in many mythic tales, an ambivalent fruit – the apple – is set before the heroine. She must choose whether to eat or forego the temptation. The risk of evil is inherent in the possibility of experience, whether that is sex, love, enterprise, knowledge, discovery. (Kolbenschlag 1979, p. 32)

Developmentally and psychologically, Snow White moves after eating the apple from the "want for nothing" Eden of the dwarfs and her unconscious identification with the Self, into a transformative sleep from which she can emerge an individual. Theologically, it is this intentional entry into the dark night of the soul that holds the promise of Snow White's authentic connection with the Divine.

Snow White must succumb to the right temptation in order to be saved by grace. She must die to the busy "doing" world of the dwarfs and fall into the deep sleep where it's possible to connect with an authentic source of being. As British author Harry Guntrip (1969) outlines, the true self may be "hidden in cold storage awaiting a chance of rebirth. This concept may include both a regressed ego awaiting rebirth and unevoked potentialities which have never yet emerged" (p. 81). When the false self adaptation breaks down, psyche is able to descend to the mysterious void at the center. With Snow White's death and descent into the unconscious there arises the possibility of a new connection at the center.

In our culture, it is frequently our connection with "being" that is split off in the unconscious. Identity and self-esteem are too often based solely on what we do, what we accomplish. Harry Guntrip, as well as many depth-psychologists, identify this living sense of being with the feminine principle. Without a living connection to one's center of being, we're easily caught in false-self doing and self-esteem striving. Speaking of this split-off quality theoretically, Guntrip states:

> It is always the female element that we find dissociated, in both men and women, and that the fundamental dissociation is of the female element. If "being" exists, "doing" will follow naturally from it. If it is not there but dissociated, then a forced kind of "doing" will have to do duty for both. (ibid., p. 253)

It is this living connection with being that allows us to feel real. It is this living connection with being that allows us to love.

Speaking metaphorically about this dynamic in terms of a woman patient, Guntrip states:

> The loving heart of her has fled from the scene, has regressed deep within, and she has lost her true self without which she cannot form living ties. (ibid., p. 90)

After the third and final temptation, the dwarfs again try to revive Snow White, but this time to no avail. "They laid her upon a bier, and all seven of them sat round it and wept for her, wept three days long." They place her in a glass coffin and stay to watch her. The glass coffin symbolically represents her condition, as well as that of the narcissistic personality's separation from the world, which has been there all along. Yet her tricolor image remains vibrant, maintaining the hope of rebirth. "She still looked as if she were living." Snow White's appearance of living death reminds me of the image that the narcissist emanates. Perfect but static, it is an image designed to occlude an inner deadness.

While she is in this coffin, she is visited by an owl, a raven, and a dove. These visits seem to me to be the most mysterious moments of the story and represent its turning point. These birds symbolize the processes of transformation that occur in the heroine while she is thought to be dead. It is after their visits that the prince arrives. Symbolically, the owl is a bird associated with death, darkness, despair, passivity, coldness, and ignorance. "It pertains to the realm of the dead sun. The sun which has set below the horizon and is crossing the lake or sea of darkness" (Cirlot 1962, p. 257).

The owl's nest has the constant smell of carrion. Yet the owl is "also an attribute of Christ who went into Darkness to save the souls in dark Hell in order to return as Light of the World" (deVries 1974, p. 353). In addition, the owl inhabits the death islands of both Athene and Calypso. The dynamic energy of the warrior goddess of commerce, craft, and strategy and the alluring energy of the siren could be useful to Snow White in her quest for wholeness. In terms of a soul's maturation, an attitude of naivete, overly sentimental spirituality, and/or childlike passive-dependence on one's creator could be broken down, energized, and empowered by the archetypal energy carried by Athene and Calypso.

The symbolism of the raven is even darker. It bodes death and brings contagion. It is a scavenger with the attributes of hardness and cruelty. It represents undifferentiated darkness, the rage and sadism that fuel envy. Alchemically, the raven is a symbol of the *nigredo*, the darkest moment in the alchemical process (Cirlot 1962; deVries 1974). The raven is the bird that Noah first sent out from the ark to find out if the rain had stopped. But the raven found a floating corpse and began to eat it. When it did not return, Noah sent out a dove which returned with muddy feet, signaling that there was land ahead.

In another parallel to the Flood story, the dove now appears at Snow White's coffin. After the descent of the owl and the raven, the dove appears to herald her resurrection. The dove is a Christian symbol for the Holy Ghost, the feminine aspect of Divine Wisdom, Sophia. In terms of the archetypal feminine, the dove is sacred to Aphrodite, Athene, Astarte, and the Virgin Mary. Alchemically, a dove is seen as contained in lead, an image that is interpreted as spirit embedded in matter (Cirlot 1962). The dove is a symbol of baptism, spiritual rebirth, and the cleansing of original sin.

In the Flood story, the dove signals the end of the night sea journey by returning to the ark after making connection with the living earth. I imagine here that the dove announces Snow White's reunion with her split-off sense of being.

In "Little Snow White" it is only after the dove's visit that the prince arrives. As well, the dissolution of the false self frees the positive animus, who rescues Snow White back into life. Again, unlike the Disney version, here the heroine is not awakened by a kiss. Rather, as the Prince's servants stumble while carrying away her coffin, the poisonous red apple is dislodged from her throat and she revives. I'd like to think that the connection with the Self announced by the dove has freed the positive animus, which is then able to dislodge the ingested bad object. Note here that it is only dislodged, it is not yet assimilated or integrated.

I find it interesting that the apple has gotten stuck in Snow White's throat and not in her stomach. The throat is the location of the fifth chakra, which is symbolically the location of Logos, the Word. We could say that meaningful speech has been blocked by this unassimilated introject. Many women find that being able to articulate what is most important to them is an important adult achievement.

Snow White participates in her transformation by reaching out for what she desires. In doing so, she must die to her life as she knows it. In this death she is transformed by powers greater than she. Jung asserts that the experience of the Self occurs through gendered imaging: ". . . the divine form in a woman is a woman, as in a man it is a man" (1974, p. 456). The fairy tale leaves to our imagination the form in which the Self appears to Snow White.

The transformation that occurs through the action of desire and the experience of death is eloquently described by contemporary poet Ntozake Shange (1977):

> i fell into a numbness
> til the only tree i cd see
> took me up in her branches
> held me in the breeze
> made me dawn dew
> that chill at daybreak
> the sun wrapped me up swingin rose light everywhere
> the sky laid over me like a million men
> i waz cold / i waz burnin up / a child
> and endlessly weavin garments for the moon
> wit my tears
> i found god in myself
> and i loved her / i loved her fiercely

Once a proper soul connection to the Self has been made, Snow White can become the true bride. The prince here has no deed or task to perform, no tests to pass. He need only fall in love with and reach out for Snow White. This mirrors the longing and reaching out that put Snow White into the death sleep in the first place. First differentiated and now united, feminine ego and masculine animus are able to proceed to their wedding, the symbolic *hieros gamos.* "Indeed, it can be said with truth that every fairy tale that deals with a beautiful heroine and a lordly hero is speaking to us of love, is laying down patterns and examples for all our human loving" (Travers 1975, p. 62).

However, archetypal darkness is not banished from this kingdom in the tale's end. At the wedding in the Grimms' version, the witch is not allowed to disappear into the woods but is forced at the wedding to dance to her death in red-hot iron shoes. This persecutory figure dies a cruel death, her narcissistic standpoint toward reality is cruelly broken up. Her death initiates a process which allows Snow White to integrate and bear both the negative and positive poles of the archetypal feminine.

Iron is the one metal not sacred to the Great Goddess. It was thought to be imported "from abroad by foreigners" (deVries 1974). It holds connotations of punishment, cruelty, and bondage. Shoes on the other hand symbolize the vulva, fertility, and life (deVries 1974). Dancing to death in shoes of iron is a very paradoxical way to die! Paradox is the nature of the center, the Self. Perhaps the dark queen's death is no more contrary than the elements that constitute Aphrodite's birth. From the sea, the goddess of love arises, made of the stuff of her father Chronos' severed genitals. The essence of the nature of desire, death, and transformation exist in the paradoxical realm of mystery.

## REFERENCES

Bettleheim, B. 1977. *The Uses of Enchantment.* New York: Vintage Books.

Cirlot, J. E. 1962. *A Dictionary of Symbols.* London: Routledge, Paul, and Kegan.

deVries, A. 1974. *Dictionary of Symbols and Imagery.* Amsterdam: North Holland Publishing Company.

Grimm, the Brothers. 1944. *The Complete Grimm's Fairy Tales.* New York: Pantheon. Reprint Random House, 1972.

Guntrip, H. 1969. *Schizoid Phenomena, Object Relations, and the Self.* New York: International Universities Press.

Jung, C. G. 1974. *The Vision Seminars.* Zurich: Spring Publications.

Kolbenschlag, M. 1979. *Kiss Sleeping Beauty Good-bye.* Toronto: Bantam Books.

Miller, A. 1981. *The Drama of the Gifted Child.* R. Ward, trans. New York: Basic Books.

Schwartz-Salant, N. 1982. *Narcissism and Character Transformation.* Toronto: Inner City Books.

Sexton, A. 1960. The double image. In *To Bedlam and Part Way Back.* New York: Houghton, Mifflin Co.

Shange, N. 1977. *For Colored Girls Who Have Considered Suicide When the Rainbow Is Enuf.* New York: Macmillan Publishing Co.

Travers, P. L. 1975. *About the Sleeping Beauty.* New York: McGraw-Hill.

Walker, B. G. 1983. *The Woman's Encyclopedia of Myths and Secrets.* San Francisco: Harper & Row Publishers.

Winnicott, D. W. 1965. Ego distortion in terms of true and false self. In *The Maturational Processes and the Facilitating Environment.* New York: International Universities Press.

# "The Tsar, His Son, and the Swan Princess"
# Men in the Hands of Women

## Joel Ryce-Menuhin

In 1905, the Progress Publishers of Moscow published a delight-
fully illustrated edition of a fairy tale by Alexander Pushkin.
With drawings by I. Bilibin, it was dedicated to the composer N.
Rimsky-Korsakov and translated from the Russian by Louis Zol-
likoff in 1970 for a new edition. Its title reads, "The Tale of Tsar
Saltan, of His Son, the Glorious and Mighty Knight, Prince Guidon Saltanovitch, and of the Fair Swan Princess." In this paper,
which is a tale within a tale, I shall be considering the power of
women in both their light and dark aspects.

### The Tsar, His Son, and the Swan Princess

T he First Night

> "My little son, it is past your bedtime and you should soon fall
> asleep, but first I'll tell you a fairy tale as told to me by a black cat!
> This cat purred and meowed that one evening three youthful sisters
> were sitting by a log fire in their cottage fantasizing 'were our tsar to
> marry me. . . .'"

The eldest sister claimed she would make the tsar wonderful
royal feasts while the second of the three would weave him superb
cloth of gold for the royal wardrobe.

Little did the youngest of the three know what fate (which for most, my son, is usually not a friendly word) had led the tsar himself to listen to the conversation outside their cottage door, when she said, "I would give our tsar an heir—handsome, brave, beyond compare." These words made the tsar's heart beat, he opened their door and proposed to the youngest sister on the spot. He married her the same December night and a son was conceived to be born the following September.

But the whirlwind marriage was not the only whirlwind to come. Foreign wars took Tsar Saltan to the front lines of battle. When his lusty son was born back at the palace, the tsar's mother-in-law, the elder sister, and the second sister of the tsaritsa kidnapped the messenger sent to the front with the glad tidings for the tsar. Instead a message was given to Tsar Saltan that the heir to the throne was neither male nor female but a hideous freak! Although the tsar sent back a message not to do anything about this dynastic disaster until he returned from the wars, the two elder sisters and their mother got the returning messenger drunk and so substituted this message:

"Have the queen and have her spawn

Drowned in secret 'ere the dawn."

The courtiers sealed the queen's fate, so they thought, by putting mother and child in a tarred, sealed casket and casting it into the sea.

However, the baby son, Prince Guidon Saltanovitch, had *magic* powers! He grew up in only one night and talked to the waves on which the barrel tossed, asking them to bring the barrel to safety on dry land. And so the waves relented and pushed the casket gently to shore. The lusty prince merely knocked and pushed his head through the wooden barrel to make a door for his mother, the queen, to step out onto the beach of an island paradise.

*"Ah, you doze off, my little sweet son, so I can ponder to myself. . . ."*

Here, an absent father, betrayed by a jealous mother-in-law and her two elder spinster daughters, has a "superbaby" son, capable alone of saving his mother and himself from treachery. A hunter and gatherer from the start, the youthful prince made a bow of an oak branch and took the silken cord from his neck, on which hung a cross, to string a bow. Shaping an arrow from a reed, the prince went about the island looking for game.

*"But you are asleep, my son. I shall think no more tonight of this tale. . . ."*

## The Second Night

*"It is late, soon you must sleep, my son. But first I'll tell you more
of the fairy tale I heard from the black cat. . . ."*

One day at the beach, Prince Guidon heard a swan honking in
distress as an eagle made ready to dive, talons spread, to kill it.
Prince Guidon shot the eagle in the throat with his bow and arrow
and so severely wounded the predator that it fell into the water
weakly flapping about. The swan attacked with beak and wings and
killed the eagle, which sank into the sea.

> Then the swan, in Russian accents, murmured:
> "O, tsarevich, champion peerless,
> My deliverer so fearless
> Grieve not that because of me
> Your good shaft is in the sea;
> That you'll have to fast three morrows
> This is but the least of sorrows.
> Your kind deed I will repay.
> I will serve you too, one day;
> 'Tis no swan that you set free,
> But a maiden charmed, you see;
> 'Twas a wizard, not a kite,
> That you slew, O noble knight;
> I shall ne'er forget your deed
> Now go back and take your rest
> All will turn out for the best."

The swan telling this then flew away.
*"Ah, you doze off, my beautiful son, so I can ponder this tale.
. . ."*
The hunter son and his dependent mother then stumbled upon
the swan's first gift, a golden spacious city waiting for Prince Guidon to rule it, where before there had been only a plain with one
oak tree upon it. When merchants came over the waters in their
ships to visit the prince's city-state, he asked them where they
would sail next. He learned they were putting out to visit his
father's land, which made him pensive, wishing once more to meet
his unknown sire. The swan magically turned the prince into a
mosquito so he could stow away on the merchant ship.
Reaching Tsar Saltan, the merchant described the beauteous
city and the compliments sent by Prince Guidon. The tsar didn't
know the mosquito prince looked on as his eldest sister, who was

royal cook, made fun of the new glorious city-state and of the prince's invitation to the tsar to visit it one day. The mosquito in fury stung all the sight forever from his aunt's right eye. But the story she told in jest that Prince Guidon had a squirrel cracking nuts that became golden-shelled kernels of precious emerald stones turned out to be true! For when the prince, turned into a royal person again, asked his swan maiden about this upon his return home, she granted him great wealth as each nut became a golden-covered emerald and the city grew rich in treasure.

*"Now my little, treasured son, you are so sleepy. Tomorrow night, I'll tell you how the prince became a tiny fly! And even a wasp! Lights out, my sleepyhead. Sweet dreams. . . ."*

The Third Night

*"Now be quiet and good, my son, as I tell you more of the tale I heard from the friendly black cat. . . ."*

More sea merchants arrived at Prince Guidon's shore, sailing back from there to his father's land. When they arrived they told the tsar of the gold coins being minted from the squirrel's golden nuts in the bright, shining city of the prince. When the prince's aunt, the royal weaver, told a story that thirty-three stalwart knights would appear after a tidal wave hit Prince Guidon's shore, the prince, whom the swan had turned into a fly so he could visit his father's court, stung the weaver's left eye of all of its sight. Then the fly flew back to his own domain and indeed, thirty-three knights, led by Chernomor, their chief, came out of the huge breakers, crashing from the sea like thunder. They were all actually brothers of the swan maiden.

The prince became a wasp to visit his father's court once more. The tsar's mother-in-law predicted a charming princess would wed the prince soon. Exasperated at this effrontery, the wasp stung his evil grandmother's nose, raising huge red and white blisters that were so poisonous her immune system failed to heal her hideous fce forever more.

Then the wasp flew back home. He turned back into Prince Guidon and asked the swan for a princess bride. The swan transformed herself at once into his perfect princess and they consummated their marriage straight away! The prince then invited his father, the tsar, to visit, and this time the old man did come. This fourth invitation could not be stopped by the wicked, jealous women who tried to break the tsar's personal happiness.

As the tsar and his retinue arrived, Prince Guidon led them toward the golden city:

> "Now the palace came in sight.
> Sentries, clad in armor bright.
>
> . . . .
>
> Further on the guests now press,
> Meet the wonderful princess;
> In her braids, a crescent beams,
> On her brow, a bright star gleams;
> She is fair of form and face,
> Full of majesty and grace.
> Tsar Saltan's own wife beside her,
> He gazed on and recognized her.
> And his heart began to leap;
> "Am I dreaming in my sleep?"
> Gasped the tsar in start surprise,
> Tears a-streaming from his eyes.
> He embraced his wife in pride,
> Kissed his son, his son's fair bride;
> Then they all sat down to feast
> Where their laughter never ceased.
>
> . . . .
>
> Late at night, with tipsy head,
> Tsar Saltan was put to bed.
> I drank beer and mead there – yet
> Only got my whiskers wet."

*"So, my son, we have a happy ending. Now off goes the light and I wish you happy dreams this night. . . ."*

The Fourth Night

*"Son, you were so active today, you have fallen asleep before I carried you up to bed. While you dream of me telling you a fairy tale, let me interpret psychodynamically what an adult might see in the darker side of the tale told me by the black cat. . . ."*

MATRIARCHY

In primitive Russia, matriarchy in family life has held sway in settling the marriages of children for generations. There is a strict order observed: the eldest of either gender must marry first, then the second, then the third. When in our fairy tale the tsar proposed to the third daughter, overlooking the older two, he so offended the mother's tradition of power in arranging marriage that she determined to bring the royal house down by murdering her own daugher in the casket thrown out to sea. Later, when the prince, disguised as a wasp, makes his third trip to witness his sire's court, the matriarch as a black *witch* predicts his marriage to the swan maiden. Matriarchs at best are glorified marriage brokers. Their husbands are often weak or dead at an early age, leaving the personal destiny of their children to the witch mother – out of their own unhappiness and cruel disinterest, presumably. Power in Russian households is handed to the matriarch without reserve. In this fairy tale that fact makes each family member unhappy for at least two decades!

I once treated a patient who was born the third child of a Russian matriarchal woman who hadn't wanted a third pregnancy. The house was draped throughout in black funeral swathes before the baby returned from the hospital, denoting to the father and the two older siblings that a ritual death had occurred – the healthy birth of a third offspring! Thus the mother ritually and schizophrenically signified a murder of the unwanted third, another example of psychotic matriarchal power like the evil, thwarted mother witch in the fairy story.

## THE KABIR CONNECTION

In Prince Guidon we have a simultaneous hero, for he "saves" his mother in the casket through magic and through phallicism. The sexual implications of the Oedipal mother/son relationship are forthright in the fairy tale. "He [the prince] grew up in one night . . . the *lusty* prince merely knocked and pushed his head up through the wooden barrel [or casket] to make a door for his mother, the queen, to step out into the beach of an island paradise." Well, the lusty prince acquired a fully grown penis in only one night! There's a precocious one for you! And what a night it was in the dark cavern of the barrel – or the penetration of his mother's vagina as he knocked (knocked up the lady) and pushed his head (his penis's swollen head) through the ceiling (penetration to the back of the vulva beyond the clitoris) where the queen could step out (come to multiple orgasms in steps) onto the beach (the subliminal area between the unconscious waters or vaginal fluids, and the conscious protruding landscape, or the son's mighty erection) into a paradise (sexually contented exhaustion).

The underside of Russian fairy stories usually contains sexual wildness metaphorically, and Pushkin does not disappoint the reader, as *voyeur*, in his tale. No wonder the swan maiden bides her time before trying to seduce the prince after his sexual start in "saving" his mother. She also was sexually frustrated because the tsar had long been at the war fronts when the story began. So the son's phallus is used as a ritual phallus replacing the father. In this case the son saves the thrusting casket (coital movements) by reaching dry land or the end of orgasms when no more semen or ovum is left to wash over the united seuxal organs.

One is reminded here of the *Kabeiror* or *Cabeiri* (plural of *Kabir*), who were deities of Phrygian origin thought to be the "mighty ones" because they are depicted on Greek vases as cult figures. They are pygmies with huge penises, or, metaphorically, our prince as a newborn baby suddenly with a "grown up" erection in one night of life!

The Kabir is a small, dark manikin figure of Telesphoros, a boy genius of healing who accompanies Asklepios, a demigod worshipped as the supreme physician in Greece and Rome. Telesphoros is depicted as a child in a cloak carrying a lantern to point the way. These manikins or Kabeiror were kept in a *kist, cistern, cist*, or *kistoaen*, which denote a chest, coffin, or small barrellike container. Daniel Noel (1974) writes that in the mystery cults of ancient Greece "there was a ritual utensil called a *cista mystica* or secret basket, a basket of mystery — so named because its contents were hidden. The sources indicate, however, that the contents were probably snakes and possibly representations of the phallus" (pp. 230-231). In the Thorvalder Museum, Copenhagen, there is a statue of Telesphoros with a phallus inside it, found by removing the top.

The veiled Kabir then is hidden in a basket (like the penis and testicles hidden but bulging in the tights of sportsmen or male ballet dancers, popularly called their "baskets") and is a coffinlike place disguising phallic presence and power. The *kiska* or container for keeping the kabir or phallic object might be likened also to the vulva/vagina, veiling and tightly containing the place of sexual arousal.

At a symbolic level we can say that the ordeal of incarceration in a casket set to sea brings the mother/son fusion to fruition through the son's desire to both save and be saved. In the fairy tale, the prince does later — like the Kabirian primeval swan —

elevate his crude male principle toward a higher union with a winged femininity, or the swan princess herself.

## A FAMILY AFFAIR

With the prince's marriage to the swan princess, the ground is laid for the prince's *unconscious* permission to be given to his father, the tsar, to reunite with his mother, whom presumably the tsar had thought long dead. So we have a sense of a double marriage blocked until the son/prince achieves his anima goal; the soul image projected onto an actual woman who is his peer. Hence his attention is shifted at last from mother as former anima to princess bride as new anima and future source of animation. What is still so noteworthy is the power of matrilineal line in family life, for, without the repeated magical intervention of the swan, her encouragement of the prince's actions in visiting his father's court as an insect with plenty of sting, and the metamorphosis of the swan into the perfect anima princess, Prince Guidon might be incestuously protecting only his mother. Of course the entire golden city-state, its wealth and armed forces, were also the gift of the swan princess. She is the source of power, the next supreme matriarchal queen of the world of Russian imagination.

*Pushkin repeatedly hands the sword of change to women in this tale of woe and splendor.* If the swan is a white witch, then the tsar's mother-in-law is the black witch, with the tsarina a kind of helpless, incestuous son-lover who finally, in bedding again with the tsar, puts a seal of dignity on a romping naughty tale of willpower gone mad. And isn't this tale like many family stories today where "women rule, OK?"

*"Sleep on, my son, for you have not heard my adult thoughts about the tale I learned from a black cat and you do not yet realize that you are the heir to the throne of the golden city-state yourself! When you wake up, perhaps it will be time to tell you my name is more than "papa." For my name is Prince Guidon Saltanovitch and this is the story of your inheritance. But dream on, my little prince, a while longer, my precious swanlet, my very own magical son, my very own prince. And soon, I shall buy you a black cat of your very own. And his name shall be Pushkin!"*

## REFERENCES

Noel, D. C. 1974. Veiled Kabir: C. G. Jung's phallic self-image. In *Spring 1974*, pp. 224–42.

## *"Cinderella"*
# Emergence from Ashes:
# A Borderline Process

## Jacqueline J. West

In the first volume of *Psyche's Stories,* Anne Baring analyzed the ever-popular tale of "Cinderella" from an archetypal perspective. Her analysis is quite fascinating and compelling, as amplifications of the archetypal realm so frequently can be. With reference to gnostic, Egyptian, and Sumerian myths, Baring concludes that "Cinderella"

> "is the story of the soul's "descent" into the manifest world, her loss of memory of her divine origin, her quest for understanding of herself and her relationship to the divine "source" or "world" from which she had emanated and to which, in full knowledge of who she is, she may return. . . . The tale of Cinderella tells the story of the soul's transfiguration as she is changed from soot-blackened drudge into radiant bride. (Baring 1991, pp. 62–63)

While Baring elaborates upon how the soul's descent, return, and royal marriage are rooted in mythology, I will describe how this eternal story of the soul's transformation may appear within the process of analysis. From this clinical perspective, I will show that "Cinderella" presents an initial profile of and a path of healing for women with borderline personality disorders.* When the imagery of the story is related to clinical theory and case material, it becomes evident that this fairy tale addresses how the archetypal affects, specifically envy and rage, which so frequently are associated with borderline states, may become integrated. The processes that occur within an analysis then can be seen as an individual expression, an incarnation, of the fairy story.

I will base my analysis and discussion of "Cinderella" on an adaptation of the version presented by the Brothers Grimm (Hunt et. al, 1972, pp. 121–128). Although dynamics involving rage and envy are present in all variations of the Cinderella story, including the Perrault rendition Baring emphasizes, it is my impression that their expression and resolution are most clearly depicted in the Grimm version, a synopsis of which follows.

## Cinderella

C inderella's widowed father remarried a vain woman who had two evil daughters. From then on, Cinderella was forced to do all the difficult and dirty housework, to wear only rags, and to sleep by the hearth amongst the ashes. Once, when the father returned from a trip with a tree branch that Cinderella had requested, she planted it upon her mother's grave and watered it with her tears.

One day the king announced plans for a festival to last three days, which would be held for the purpose of finding a bride for the prince. The stepsisters were thrilled and immediately put Cinderella to work on their gowns. When Cinderella asked to go also, her stepmother agreed—but only on the condition that Cinderella sort out the dish of lentils which the stepmother had thrown into the ashes. Cinderella called upon the birds who lived in the tree that had grown on her mother's grave, and they helped her accomplish this task. But no sooner was it done, than the stepmother demanded Cinderella sort two dishes of lentils out of the ashes. Again, with the help of the birds, she succeeded. Still, her evil stepmother insisted that, because she had nothing to wear but

---

*Many of these dynamics could be extended into an analysis applicable to male borderline patients who are also struggling with severe negative mother and inadequate and attacking father complexes. However, for the sake of clarity and brevity, I will restrict this discussion to the psychology of women.

filthy rags, Cinderella could not go to the ball. Bereft, Cinderella went to her mother's grave and cried out to the tree to throw down some silver and gold. And so it was that she received the glorious gown and slippers in which she arrived at the ball. Naturally, the prince chose her as his partner. When the night ended and he accompanied her home, she disappeared into a pigeon house, which her father cut down for the bewildered prince. Cinderella meanwhile had left the house, given her gowns back to the birds in the tree, and returned to her position by the hearth. The second night went much the same. But at the end of the third night, as Cinderella left the palace, her slipper got caught in some pitch the prince had spread upon the steps. After Cinderella, missing one shoe, had fled, the prince announced a search, declaring that the maiden whose foot this slipper fit would become his wife.

When the prince and his search party arrived at Cinderella's house each stepsister tried to cut down her foot down to a size that would fit into the slipper. However, as the prince left with each false bride, the birds in the tree alerted him that this was not the true bride, and he returned her to her mother. Finally, he inquired whether there was another daughter living in the house and Cinderella was summoned. Her foot fit the slipper perfectly. As the prince left with his true bride, the birds from the tree flew down to her shoulders and stayed there. During the wedding procession, the birds pecked out the eyes of the wicked stepsisters, punishing them with blindness for their evil ways.

INTERPREATION

The opening of this tale is so critical to its analysis that a detailed reveiw of it is in order. It begins with the following complex images:

As the wife of a rich man lay dying, her parting instructions to her beautiful, only daughter were for the girl to remain good and pious. Winter snows came and by spring, the girl's father had taken a new wife who had two daughters. These girls were also beautiful but were mean and evil. They insisted that their stepsister do all the difficult and dirty housework and that she wear only rags and wooden shoes. They emptied peas and lentils into the ashes so she would have to sort them out and then, with mocking voices, they called her Cinderella because she was always dusty and dirty from sleeping in the cinders by the hearth.

As Cinderella's mother dies, she instructs her daughter to be good and pious. A mother's daughter, Cinderella has lived a rich and good life but it has been noticeably one-sided. Her mother is now dying. Jung explains that "when an extreme, one-sided tendency dominates conscious life, in time an equally powerful counterposition is built up [and eventually] breaks through the conscious control" (Jung 1971, par. 709). This may result in "the transformation of the hitherto valued into the worthless, and of the former good into the bad" (ibid., par. 455). This conversion of one extreme into its opposite, a process referred to by Jung as *enantiodromia*, is certainly at work in this tale. This daughter who was raised to experience a one-sided, pleasant, supportive, and positive life is plunged suddenly into a miserable, cruel, and negative existence. Powerfully and succinctly, within only the first few sentences of the tale, we are informed of a profound conversion of good to evil, pious to profane, rich to poor, kind to cruel, white to black.

This initial conversion of opposites introduces us to the psychological dynamics of this story. The image of a girl once well-off now abandoned and beleaguered and living in rags amongst the ashes is the hallmark of the Cinderella story. This is an image of a personality in severe distress. Interpersonally suffering from abandonment, Cinderella is in a subservient role through which her true self cannot shine. Her real value is neither exhibited to nor seen by those around her. Intrapsychically, the unempowered ego – the all "good" Cinderella – is being attacked by highly negative and aggressive aspects of the psyche that are all "bad." When a person's true self lies deeply hidden behind such a ruthless battle between radically split opposites of the psyche, that person exists in a state that we call "borderline."

The term "borderline" was first used to refer to an intermediate category of pathology falling between the familiar neuroses and milder character disorders on one side, and psychosis on the other. Through the years, there has been some amount of dissatisfaction among clinicians with how diffusely this term is employed. However, the *DSM-III* now presents detailed criteria for employing the diagnosis of "Borderline Personality Disorder" and thereby helps to differentiate it from other pathologies. Among the characteristics of this disorder, the *DSM* notes a tendency toward unstable and intense relationships characterized by inappropriate and intense affect. "Cinderella" presents such a story. However, what is often questioned is whether such instability and intensity are fundamentally characteristics of a narcissistic disorder. Nathan Schwartz-Salant teases out the differences between borderline and narcissistic disorders by contrasting the ways they employ idealization and contain exhibitionistic energies. The relationship of a woman with borderline personality disorder to exhibitionism is of particular relevance to the exploration of Cinderella since, as noted above, when Cinderella is living amongst the ashes her true self is neither exhibited to nor seen by those around her; it is lost to her as well as others. Schwartz-Salant explains that exhibitionistic energies are dangerous for borderline patients because of their extreme vulnerability to emotional flooding (Schwartz-Salant 1989, p. 62). They therefore tend to split off from exhibitionism and thereby deny themselves this critical source of development. As a result, they are left with "little of a genuine, functioning self" (ibid., pp. 64–65). Cinderella is certainly in such distress.

Schwartz-Salant also suggests that borderline patients are characterized by "the splitting of ego and object into all-good and all-bad states" and that they are "enmeshed in psychic levels of extreme intensity that bear intimate relation to many of the great archetypal themes in history – battles between God and the devil and life and death" (ibid., pp. 28, 13). The process of splitting, as a primitive defense and as a defining characteristic of borderline pathology, has been given considerable attention over the past few years (cf, Abend, Porter, and Willick 1983, pp. 159ff). The earlier theories of Klein and Kernberg – which detail how the child develops good and bad internal objects through the use of internalization, splitting, and projective identification – have been modified and extended by Jungians such as Michael Fordham and Schwartz-Salant to include archetypal theory. In line with these theories, "Cinderella" can be viewed both developmentally and intrapsychically in terms of borderline dynamics.

Seen from a developmental perspective, "Cinderella" is the story of a young girl whose mother has not helped her mediate the polarities of the archetypes. Good and evil, black and white, etc., are the opposite poles of archetypal realities; they are absolutes, unmodified by effective, human, good-enough interactions. Cinderella's mother, presumably because of her own unresolved internal splits, has left Cinderella with the enormous task of learning to survive and hold the tensions of the opposites.

Seen from an intrapsychic perspective, "Cinderella" is the story of a personality wrestling with severe dissociations. From this perspective, the various characters in the story are seen as representations of different parts of the personality. These parts are a good but no longer living mother figure, a bad mother figure, an ineffectual father figure, a good girl, and two evil stepsisters. Cinderella herself, the protagonist, may be seen as the ego that has been informed only by the good mother; she has identified with and has become identified by the good. The bad—i.e., the aggressive and dark aspects of the psyche—have been split off and are now attacking the ego, which faces the arduous task of encountering and integrating "the other." Cinderella must confront the envious and raging bad mother as well as the bad sisters who represent Cinderella's shadow. Both the negative mother and the shadow present themselves as formidable complexes organized around only the negative, split-off pole of the archetype at their core. It becomes apparent that Cinderella, the ego, must find a way to tame or integrate these ruthless complexes. In his study of the problem of envy, Murray Stein notes that from a Jungian point of view, envy "is thought of as linked to the drive for individuation . . . as a symptom of a thwarted drive toward psychic wholeness" (Stein 1990, p. 163). The enantiodromia that Cinderella has suffered and must wrestle with—the conversion of the good to the bad and the eruption of envy and rage—thus may be seen as the psyche's presentation of the opposite in order to move toward wholeness. The resolution of this opposition and the development of healthy exhibitionism become the point of this fairy tale—as well as of an analysis with a borderline patient. Thus as the tale proceeds, it presents not only a profile of but a pattern of healing for the borderline personality.

Before examining how this resolution emerges in the tale, examples of how borderline people typically appear as they enter analysis will root this story in the analytic process. Borderline patients, as noted, are characterized by their marked inability to withstand the tension between the opposites. This inability frequently is related to the mother complex, and these patients therefore tend to enter analysis dominated by either the good or the bad mother. They may enter just as the good mother is dying, as in the fairy tale, or they may enter already in the grips of the negative mother.

If the good mother is just dying, it is often difficult to diagnose the underlying personality pattern; their mother's "death" may or may not be followed immediately by the sort of enantiodromia that reveals a borderline structure. Indeed, I have worked with several women for a number of months, even a couple of years, before their rage and envy attacks emerged in full force. In each case, during this initial period there were few clues that their underlying stucture was borderline. One woman, for example, entered analysis confused about her feelings toward her mother whom she had previously dearly loved. She recognized that only recently she had wanted to be under her mother's wing; however, now she wanted her own life. She was frightened and surprised that she was beginning to get angry at her mother. I could sense that the safe world of the good mother no longer sustained her, no longer had sufficient answers. This patient had lived an emotionally restricted life; in essence, she had remained the beautiful and good daughter of a good mother supported by a rich husband. But now the good mother was under seige. In the tale, the good mother dies. There was grief – winter came. And just so, this patient moved into a rather severe depression. She herself was familiar with the story of Demeter and Persephone and she began to reflect upon how her separation from her mother felt like the cruel interruption of the naive and blissful union between this mythological mother and daughter. In the myth the similarly enmeshed mother-daughter union is shattered when Persephone picks the flower upon the Eleusinian fields. Persephone is swept away to the underworld, into the realm of the unconscious. Similarly in "Cinderella," as spring arrives the naive young girl, cut off from her mother, is cast into a veritable hell; she is confronted by those aspects of the unconscious that previously have not been expressed. With spring, the new elements in the psyche arrived, not as spring flowers but as "gifts" of the underworld, the dark side of the soul. For my patient, as well as for Persephone and Cinderella, the severing of the preexisting bond with the mother felt terribly cruel, yet clearly the one-sided and undeveloped nature of the ego wedded to the good mother was untenable. As my patient wrestled with her grief and depression, she realized that she felt deeply abandoned. Because her personal mother had not helped her confront and integrate the power of the negative pole of the mother archetype, my patient was unable to tolerate the tension of the opposites. Thus, in effect, she had been abandoned. She worked with her feelings of abandonment for quite some time and then slowly her rage began to mount. Soon she found herself in the midst of fierce storms of rage. At this point she resembled patients who enter analysis already besieged.

To enter analysis already besieged is to enter after the good mother has died, that is, once the negative mother and evil sisters are seated in court. At this point intrapsychically, the ego is under attack by the negative mother and the shadow; it is in essence smeared with ashes. In the fairy tale, the sisters/shadow elements are making their presence known; they clearly now have the upper hand. For the patient, this means being at the mercy of covert or overt rage and envy attacks. These sieges generally are brought into analytical hours as accounts of attacks upon the analysand by other women, as rage and envy towards others, and intrapsychically as fierce attacks upon the self. As the transference becomes activated, these powerful, archetypal affects find their expression directly within the analytic interaction.

Whether the rage and envy are expressed interpersonally or intrapsychically, this tends to be a very stormy process, one that is extraordinarily difficult for both analysand and analyst. The affects arrive with true archetypal power and overwhelm consciousness. In so doing they often throw the analysand into a terrifying void, into that space that lies beyond description. From within this void, the analysand tends to attack and invade the analyst. It may feel as if an entire troop of demons has swept through the room. The raw and brutal power of such affects can enter and confuse the analyst, pushing her to act them out toward the patient in retaliation. It is incumbent upon the analyst to see, understand, and neither flee from nor act out this state of madness. It is particularly critical that the analyst not shame the patient for her fragmentation, disintegration, or outbursts; these intense states are the patient's full identity at those moments.

However, as critical as it is for the analyst to witness and truly accept these states, over time it becomes clear that only receiving these affects is not sufficient to transform them. Indeed, it frequently happens that rounds of strong affect have been met, endured, and even painstakingly integrated into what feels like effective interaction and increasing consciousness, yet the person remains in the grip of repeated rage and envy attacks. Why do we not see more therapeutic improvements from such intense and reflective encounters? And, given that changes do not appear, what can be done? The story of Cinderella helps to answer these questions.

Returning to the tale, we see that our protagonist, as ego, remains steady. Though she is beseiged by the negative mother and the shadow sisters, she does not react directly to them. What does she do? She chooses to strengthen her connection to the positive mother. The first step in this movement occurs one day as her father sets out on a trip.

> One day, before the father left for the fair, he asked each girl what they would like him to bring home. His stepdaughters asked for beautiful dresses, pearls and jewels, while Cinderella asked only for the first branch which knocked against her father's hat on the way home. She thus received a branch from a hazelnut tree which she then planted upon her mother's grave, watering it with her tears. The branch grew into a handsome tree beneath which Cinderella sat thrice a day, weeping and praying. There came a little white bird to the tree which threw down to Cinderella whatever she wished for.

In effect Cinderella, as ego, does not respond directly to the tyranny of the prevailing complexes that were formed around the negative pole of the mother archetype. Rather, she turns to the development of the opposite pole of the archetype, the positive mother. Building upon her earlier positive identification with the good mother, she is led to strengthen this pole of the archetype. This process is symbolized here as the growth of a magical tree rooted in her mother's grave.

Jung wrote an entire essay about the symbolism of the tree. He suggests that the tree represents a profile of the "self depicted as a process of growth" (Jung 1967, par. 304). He observes that it is commonly associated with the positive aspects of the Great Mother – the source of life, protection, shade, and nourishment (ibid., par. 350). De Vries notes that the hazel tree, along with the apple tree, is one of the most sacred of all trees and that it is related to the Great Goddess (de Vries 1974, p. 242). In some versions of Cinderella, the tree is indeed an apple tree. This tree symbolically offers knowledge, wisdom, and fertility. Thus Cinderella's decisive actions when she plants and nourishes a hazelnut tree at her mother's grave inform us symbolically that she has taken a significant step in her journey to the Self by developing her relationship to the positive Goddess. The tree and its growth foretell as well as support Cinderella's transformation.

In the comforting arms of the tree, Cinderella weeps freely. Her tears further strengthen the tree and they also strengthen her, the ego. She begins to grieve the loss she has suffered. In doing so, she moves closer to letting go of the illusion that her perfect mother could protect her from pain, the illusion that she could live in archetypal peace. She begins to experience being human. Tears, symbolically and dynamically, are recognized as having healing, redemptive, and fructifying powers (Leonard 1982, pp. 136ff). One can sense that as Cinderella weeps by the hazel tree she not only nourishes her connection to the source of life, she also strengthens her heart.

A similar movement often appears in analysis. Borderline patients are frequently possessed by their negative complexes and they therefore tend to rage and attack. In such a case, a growing ability to pause and weep is a major accomplishment, one that reflects both an increased willingness on the part of the patient to accept her humanness and also the increased development of that archetypal pole which opposes the raging. Although the rage and envy tend to be well entrenched, just as the stepmother and wicked sisters have the upper hand, once these affects are well acknowledged, moments tend to appear when grief may enter. In these newly available spaces, a choice to turn from the envy and rage no longer feels like a denial of these affects. Indeed, at this point, when the energy behind a rage or envy storm begins to mount, the patient tends to welcome the analyst's efforts to help her turn away from the rage and into the grief. The patient now is ready to learn how to pause, take a deep breath, and find a place to rest, possibly to weep. One borderline patient I worked with imagined this place as a special meadow by a stream; another, as my lap. For each, this was a place where she could curl up, rest, and weep – sometimes after, but increasingly instead of, being possessed by murderous rage or crippling envy. In essence, these patients were learning to do what Cinderella did: to water the tree with their tears instead of becoming possessed by the negative figures within themselves. In an article on modifying cruelty through human love and understanding, Eric Brenman describes how the analyst can help the patient build up a "concept of home," a psychological home within the analysis and within herself, where she is relatively free of ruthless attacks upon goodness in others and/or in herself. A critical building block of such a home is grief expressed through tears.

When Cinderella chooses to strengthen the positive mother rather than to respond directly to the attacks of the negative mother and the shadow sisters, this naturally increases the tension between the opposites. So, as one might expect, this is followed by malicious maneuvers on the part of the negative mother. These maneuvers appear to be arbitrary as well as cruel, but in effect they facilitate Cinderella's development. This occurs as follows:

One day the King announced plans for a festival which would last three days. All the young maidens in the country were invited so that the prince might choose a bride. The stepsisters were thrilled and immediately began to order Cinderella to tend to their preparations. Cinderella herself longed to go to the ball and begged her stepmother to allow her to do so. Her stepmother initially refused, cruelly emphasizing that Cinderella was far too dirty and ill-dressed to dance! However, when Cinderella persisted, the harsh woman eventually set her terms: she emptied a dish of lentils into the ashes and said that if Cinderella could pick them out within two hours, she could go along. Cinderella went into the garden and called for the tame pigeons, the turtledoves, and all the birds beneath the sky to come and help her pick

> The good into the pot,
> The bad into the crop.

Flocks of birds whirred into the kitchen and began to pick, pick, pick, gathering the good grains into the dish. They finished in less than an hour and quickly flew away. With great anticipation, Cinderella took the dish to her stepmother only to find that her stepmother was insistent that Cinderella would be laughed at because she did not have proper clothes and could not dance. When Cinderella cried, her stepmother announced: this time if you can pick two dishes of lentils out of the ashes within one hour, you can come with us. The stepmother felt smugly certain that Cinderella could not do that! When she had gone, Cinderella again went into the garden and called to the birds. And again flocks of birds whirred into the kitchen, alighted amongst the ashes, and began to pick, pick, pick, separating the good from the bad. In less than a half hour they finished and flew away. With delight, Cinderella carried the dishes to her stepmother, who announced that all her work would not help. She declared that she would be ashamed of Cinderella at the balls because she had no clothes and could not dance and she hurried off to the festival with her own two proud daughters.

The tasks set for Cinderella by the negative mother would indeed be insurmountable if they were approached in a direct and rational manner. However, Cinderella knows to call for help; she calls in the birds. Psychologically, she calls upon a form of unconscious support. Neumann presents a detailed analysis of the similar task that Aphrodite sets for Psyche; he concludes that the ants that assist Psyche in her sorting are "symbols of the instinct world"; he contrasts them to the doves that "many centuries later" come to Cinderella's help (Neumann 1952, pp. 94–95). It is quite interesting to consider why it is birds that help Cinderella. Birds are generally associated with transcendence, spirit, angels (de Vries 1974, p. 48; Cooper 1978, p. 20). And yet it seems apparent that it is an instinctual power that is guiding Cinderella, helping her to select and separate. I would suggest that the birds who help Cinderella represent an unconscious principle that is at once both instinctual and spiritual; they represent both the somatic and the psychic unconscious. In that they themselves embody a union of opposites, they are well equipped to differentiate good from bad.

The relationship between good and bad is one of the essential points of this entire fairy tale. Therefore, the tasks assigned to Cinderella by her stepmother present us with an image of the "problem" of the tale set within the tale, a story within the story. The symbolism of separating lentils from ashes is particularly intriguing. The lentils, as seeds, hold all the promise of new life. Again, we find echoes of the Demeter-Persephone story, Demeter being the Great Goddess of the seed. Cinderella, like Persephone, is a seed lost in darkness. The ashes, as the darkness, are the image of the bad. The seeds mixed up in the ashes then present us with the image of a lack of differentiation between good and bad. Therefore, as Cinderella separates the lentils from the ashes, she demonstrates her increased ability to differentiate and tolerate the tension between the opposite poles of the archetype of the Mother. While Cinderella masters this critical phase of development, it is intriguing to keep in mind that the bad is not all bad, the good not all good. This is apparent in the multidimensionality of the symbol of ashes which, as the birth place of the phoenix, suggest rebirth. We are thus led to consider the value of the bad, in this case the value of the bad mother. It was after all the demands of the stepmother that forced Cinderella to develop her powers of discrimination, just as Aphrodite's demands had directed Psyche. As Neumann emphasizes, "Psyche's course from labor to labor becomes a *way*" (Neumann 1952, p. 98). It is critical to note, however, that for both Psyche and Cinderella the completion of the assigned tasks is necessary but not sufficient.

In the case of Cinderella, her achievements are cruelly dismissed. Certainly, the stepmother is not being "fair" when she does not honor her agreements that Cinderella could go to the ball once she has completed the assigned task. That Cinderella meets her demands in and of itself does not lead to Cinderella's release, that is, to transformation. The stepmother's maliciousness makes it clear once again that it is critically important but not sufficient to meet the negative mother directly. The complex formed around the negative pole of the archetype simply continues to attack the ego ruthlessly: "You are too dirty, you cannot dance, you will embarrass me." Often a borderline analysand hears such persecutory messages play over and over again within her own mind. She may act out this persecution toward the analyst; possessed by the negative mother, the patient feels that absolutely everything the analyst does is inadequate—more than that, wrong, all wrong. Given that the analyst carries the ego function for her patient at times, the analyst becomes Cinderella, deftly sorting through the ashes for each and every lentil. And the patient possessed by the negative mother insists on more and more and then dismisses what has been done. Indeed, there is absolutely nothing that can satisfy the negative mother. In those moments, the analyst experiences the torture of the reality in which the patient lives. And, again, the question arises: What can be done when the ego, located dynamically in the patient and/or the analyst, is being ruthlessly attacked by the complexes formed around the negative pole of the archetype?

At this point in the fairy tale the ego is certainly under such an attack: Cinderella is dismissed and left at home; the bad holds sway. It is becoming more and more apparent that the potential value in the bad, the negative, can only be reaped when the bad is sufficiently balanced by the good. Thus it seems clear that what Cinderella must do is turn once more to the positive mother.

Bereft, Cinderella went to her mother's grave beneath the hazel tree and cried. She then called out,

> Shiver and quiver, little tree,
> Silver and gold throw down over me.

The bird in the tree then threw down to Cinderella a beautiful gold and silver dress and lovely slippers embroidered with silk. She dressed quickly and hurried off to the ball. Upon her arrival, she was thought to be an exotic foreign princess; she was recognized by no one. The prince was drawn to her immediately and would dance with none other for the remainder of the evening. If another asked her to dance, the prince replied that she was his partner.

This is the major turning point in the tale. After the intense onslaught by the negative mother, Cinderella turns once again to the development of the positive mother. This time by seeking and receiving the blessing from the tree, Cinderella not only strengthens the presence of the positive mother, she experiences a release from darkness. She is showered with "gold and silver." The magical and transformative power of the tree becomes amply apparent. Baring presents poetic amplifications of the heavenly beauty of Cinderella's gowns and concludes that they "symbolize the awakening and growth of wisdom which clothes the soul in ever-greater radiance" (Baring 1991, p. 60). Jung notes that the tree of paradise is often hung not with apples but with sun-and-moon fruit and, as such, is a world tree (Jung 1967, pars. 398, 405). In the most familiar stories it is a goddess-mother who plays the role of the tree and who, with a wave of her wand, transforms Cinderella's rags into riches. In these versions the positive mother is given more explicit form, though clearly she shares the same archetypal source as the tree. However, the tree with its fruits of gold maintains a closer tie to alchemical imagery. Jung studies several alchemical texts about the golden fruit of the tree and he concludes that they say, "God himself dwells in the fiery glow of the sun and appears as the fruit of the philosophical tree and thus as the opus, whose course is symbolized by the growth of the tree" (ibid., par. 404). He also notes that "the tree with the bird stands for the opus and its consummation" (ibid., par. 415).

Thus, the gift that Cinderella receives when the small bird in the tree throws down gowns of silver and gold is nothing less than the potential to reveal her true, "golden" self. This capacity arises when the opposite poles of the mother archetype find their appropriate balance in each other's strength. Once the archetypal positive mother is strengthened, it presents a viable opposition to the archetypal negative mother. The mother archetype is then experienced as bipolar, or ambivalent, and the ego can stand in relationship to it, be aligned with it, rather than be attacked or possessed by it. In effect, by creating a strong tension between the two powerful poles of the mother archetype, Cinderella ultimately sets herself free of each. She receives a golden gown, her authentic self, and is free to go to the ball.

It is, similarly, a treasured moment in analysis when a borderline person begins to seek the presence of the positive. Each time a moment of light is allowed, the crippling imbalance that lies deep within the archetypal realm is addressed. This is beautifully portrayed in the fairy tale when Cinderella asks for and receives a gift of gold and silver. Emerging from the dark, ash-smeared state, Cinderella manifests the light. This occurs in analysis when the borderline patient begins to ask for and receive a mutual relationship with the analyst. Each time the patient is accurately perceived and understood – through the analytic processes of personification of inner figures as well as through mirroring and interpretation – she can trust a little more. Emerging from hatred and envy, the patient feels a single moment of trust and love. She then becomes more able to present her relatively unpossessed, authentic, and human self; she is less a representative of the archetypal world, the collective unconscious, and more an individual. In a similar way, each time an "optimal failure" of the analyst is recognized, interpreted, and integrated, the patient has the opportunity to learn to accept the analyst as "merely" human and to trust her for that (Kohut 1984, p. 69). The analyst then begins to be seen as neither god nor devil, neither goddess-mother nor witch, neither all-good nor all-evil. Rather, she can be seen as human, as an individual, as "a good-enough mother," in Winnicott's terms (Winnicott 1971, pp. 10ff). Theoretically, the patient's experience of both herself and her analyst in more individual terms reveals a release from the grip of archetypal forces; experientially, it ushers in a sorely needed and very welcome atmosphere of humanity.

The differentiation of the good and bad archetypal mother as well as the differentiation between the archetypal and the human mother releases the patient. She now has a sufficiently clear sense of her self, her human self, that she can relate to rather than be possessed by the gods. Indeed, I have seen several borderline women discover the power of prayer as they traverse this particular development. As moments of trust and love are experienced with the analyst in a human way, a natural desire to experience this state in divine or archetypal terms seems also to arise. Thus, prayers to the Mother-Who-Provides, or to the Earth, sometimes appear. For example, one woman described how she would lie upon the ground, in a carefully chosen spot, and rest her body upon the Mother's, breathing her breath, crying her tears, feeling her pulse of life. That these developments are critical for border-line patients is supported by Schwartz-Salant's observation that, "The borderline patient is both besieged by the negative numino-sum and terrified of engaging its positive forms" (Schwartz-Salant 1989, p. 33). When the terror of the positive begins to yield, as it has when a prayer to the Earth Mother can emerge, clearly a major change has occurred in the borderline structure. The patient now is dressed in gold and silver; the light of spirit shines through her.

Cinderella in her magical gowns is capable of going to the ball and meeting the prince. She can present her true self to the world and find the animus, her soul mate. The opposite poles of the mother archetype have been sufficiently differentiated and the tension between them has been increased to the point that a "third thing," a synthesis, is formed. In analysis at this point, the patient may discover the capacity to try out her real self in the world. It is as if the analysand is granted short "breathing spells" – at least until the ball is over. But then what happens?

The next rather complicated segments of this story basically portray how Cinderella establishes a relationship between herself and the prince or, intrapsychically, between the ego and the newly found animus.

When the festival ended that night, the prince wished to accompany Cinderella to her home. However, at the last moment, she escaped from him and sprang into the pigeon house. The prince waited until Cinderella's father arrived and then told him that the unknown maiden had lept into the pigeon house. The old man wondered if the maiden were Cinderella. He fetched an ax and hewed the pigeon house into pieces, only to find that no one was inside it. Meanwhile, Cinderella had jumped down quickly from the back of the pigeon house, had run to her mother's grave where she returned the beautiful clothes to the little bird in the tree, and had returned to the hearth in the kitchen. When everyone else eventu-ally got home, they found Cinderella settled down, as usual, in her dirty clothes amongst the ashes.

The next day after her father, stepmothers, and stepsisters set off for the palace, Cinderella went directly to the the hazel tree and intoned it once again to throw down silver and gold over her.

Dressed in an even more beautiful dress, Cinderella arrived at the ball and was greeted by the King's son, who had waited for her and who, again, would have neither of them dance with another. This time when the dancing finished, the prince followed Cinderella so that he might see which home she entered. However, she sprang away from him, ran into the garden behind the house, and as nimbly as a squirrel climbed into the magnificent pear tree which grew there. Again, the prince waited until the father arrived and explained to him that the unknown maiden had quickly fled, possibly into the pear tree. The father again wondered if the maiden could be Cinderella and he proceeded to cut down the tree only to find no one there. Cinderella, naturally, had jumped down from the other side of the tree and, having returned her beautiful ball gown to the bird in the hazel tree, she had settled into her accustomed position in her grey rags amongst the ashes.

At the end of her first two evenings with the prince, Cinderella leads him back to her father's house, where she quickly "slips away." First she hides in the pigeon house, then in the pear tree. Her ineffectual father, who has never really seen her and has not valued and protected her, tries to find her in these places by hewing and chopping. Thus, through ignorance he uselessly destroys the home of birds and the fruit of nature. This is a powerful vignette in that it is a portrait of an extremely painful moment, intrapsychically and interpersonally as well as culturally.

Intrapsychically, when Cinderella leads the prince back to her father's house she "announces" that there are dynamics involving the father that have to be addressed. In effect, she leads the animus to the father complex. Thus far, I have emphasized that this is a story about the archetypal mother. However, these sections are clearly about the relation between the ego, the animus, and the father complex. The ego, now well aligned with the Self, meets the animus but cannot sustain this connection until the father is engaged. The ego thus leads the animus into the territory of the father; however, then she mysteriously flees. She returns her beautiful gowns, her true self, and once again resumes her disguise amongst the ashes. She thus introduces the prince, the animus, to the problem: her true self is neither revealed nor seen. The prince, nonetheless, has seen that there was something of great value to be found. When he suggests this to the father, the father tries to get his daughter by cutting his way into her hiding places. This is a futile and destructive act by the father complex, derived from his blindness. He does not see the value of his daughter and once this is suggested, he does not know how to approach her without cruelly cutting into a "body," into the pigeon house and the pear tree, from which she naturally had fled.

This episode is quite blatantly violent. It can be viewed as a portrait of literal, concrete relationship or as an image of the father complex. As literal relationship, it suggests that the father of the borderline patient has approached his daughter violently and abusively. As Judith Herman attests, a "great majority" of female borderline patients have "documented histories of severe childhood trauma," frequently in the form of sexual and/or physical abuse (Herman 1992, p. 126). The image in the story of the father who cuts into a "body" from which Cinderella has fled is a powerful image of a father abusing a girl who, in defense, dissociates, a girl who emotionally flees her body in order to survive.

Viewing this episode of the tale in terms of the father complex, one can witness how this complex attacks the developing self both intrapsychically and, in projected form, interpersonally. This typically occurs when a borderline patient attempts to present herself through a creative product or personally. I have worked with several borderline patients who are artists and who have each gone through extended periods of total paralysis in their work. Whenever they began to write or paint, their own attacks upon the pieces were ruthless. They were unsparing in their cutting and hewing! They also presented their work in such a way as to essentially guarantee rejection. This same process can be seen in the analytic hour when a patient gains enough courage to present her authentic self. This is often followed by an onslaught. The patient may express such an attack in terms of self-criticism. For example, she may quickly add a cutting remark about her self-exposure, such as "Oh, I'm being so immature" or "This is really trivial," etc. Such devaluations are clearly attacks by the father complex and they effectively destroy both the moment and her newly developing self. Or, the patient may experience the attack in a projected form as coming from the analyst. For example, following a moment of genuine exposure, the patient may face immediate terror that the analyst will hate and abandon her for it. As Schwartz-Salant concludes, "it would appear that the borderline person lives so close to persecutory energy fields that he or she remains chronically open to psychic dismemberment" (Schwartz-Salant 1989, p. 66). Thus the patient, like Cinderella, tends to recoil quickly from her creative act, hiding once again amongst the ashes while the father complex wreaks its havoc.

This episode of the tale may also be seen as a graphic metaphor for our cultural relationship to the vulnerable body of nature. We have been dominated culturally by a father complex that has led us to hew and chop without regard; we cut down forests and ruin natural habitats with abandon. It may well be that what we are looking for in all this frenzy has long since fled and is waiting elsewhere in disguise. It may well be that the feminine spirit has appeared in brief glimpses only to retreat, that the animus of the world is in search of her and has sparked off the father's cruel intrusions.

Given all this, what does the fairy tale tell us about what might happen next? It proceeds:

On the third day of festivities at the palace, after all the others had left, Cinderella once more sang to her tree. This time she received a gown even more splendid and magnificent than the previous two and her slippers were made of gold. Everyone at the ball was so astonished at her beauty that they fell into silence. Again the king's son would dance with no one else and insisted that she was his partner. That night as the ball ended Cinderella slipped away from the prince at the palace. The prince, however, had foreseen this and had smeared the palace steps with pitch. As Cinderella fled, her left slipper remained stuck in the pitch. The prince found the dainty, golden slipper and declared that the maiden whose foot it fit would be his wife.

On the night of the third ball, Cinderella slips away from the prince at the palace. Three is the fairy tale number of transformation, and indeed this is a moment of change. On this third night, the critical action occurs in the palace, not at Cinderella's home. The prince finally realizes that his way to Cinderella does not lie through the father and he takes matters into his own hands. This reflects a shift away from the father. Dynamically, the animus appears to be successfully wrested from the father complex. There remains, however, the question of how Cinderella, as ego, will ultimately develop her relationship to the father; this is a story told in other tales. Meanwhile, the determination of the animus to unveil the truth about Cinderella becomes evident in his move to spread pitch upon the stairs; he wants to catch the "real thing." Pitch is the sap of trees, symbolically the celestial milk of the mother goddess (de Vries 1974, p. 400). The animus thus lets Cinderella know that he is knowledgeable about the world of the goddess. Cinderella, however, is still not ready to be seen; she is able only to leave a clue, her shoe. With this clue, the prince can measure her, in essence measure the trueness of her self. The animus, no longer impeded by the father, now can proceed to investigate and measure.

When the slipper was brought to Cinderella's house, the stepsisters were eager to try it on. The eldest seized the shoe and went with her mother into her room. There she discovered that the shoe was too small; she simply could not get her toe in it. Her mother then handed her a knife and instructed her to cut off her toe. The mother assured her daughter that when she was queen she would have no need to go about on foot. The girl did as told: she cut off her toe, forced her foot into the shoe, swallowed her pain, and went out to the prince. The prince put her upon his horse and headed towards the palace. However, as they passed by the grave, the two doves sitting in the hazel tree sang out to the prince to turn and see the blood within the shoe, they sang out that the shoe was too small and that the true bride was still waiting. Seeing this truth, the prince took the false bride home. The second sister and her mother then took the golden slipper into her chamber whereupon they discovered that her heel was too large to fit into it. Handing her daughter the knife, the mother instructed her to cut a bit off her heel for, once she was queen, she would have no need to go about on foot. The daughter cut off her heel, forced her foot into the slipper, swallowed her pain, and went out to the prince. The prince lifted her upon his horse and rode away. However, once again as they passed the hazel tree at the head of the grave, the two doves sitting there sang out to the prince. They instructed him to turn and see the blood in the shoe, to see that the shoe was too small, to realize that the true bride was still waiting. When the prince turned and saw blood running from the shoe he turned his horse around and took the false bride home. He then asked the girls' father whether he had any other daughters. He replied that there was only a stunted little kitchen wench left by his previous wife, certainly not the bride. When the prince asked that she come in, the stepmother insisted that she was far too dirty to show herself. The prince nevertheless prevailed and Cinderella was summoned.

When she drew her foot out of her heavy wooden shoe and put it into the slipper it fit like a glove! The king's son then recognized his dancing partner and exclaimed that she must be his true bride. The stepmother and stepsisters were horrified and outraged as they watched the prince take Cinderella upon his horse and ride away. This time as the prince and maiden passed the hazel tree, the two doves happily sang out to the prince that there was no blood in the shoe, it fit, indeed he had found the true bride. They then flew down, sat upon Cinderella's shoulders, and remained there.

When the wedding day arrived, the two evil sisters attempted to flatter Cinderella in order to share her great fortune. They walked by her side on the way to and from the church. On the way, the doves on Cinderella's shoulder leaned over and pecked out one eye from each of the sisters; on the way home, they pecked out the remaining eye from each. In this way, the sisters were punished with blindness for their false and evil ways.

For Cinderella, delivery from the negative mother is certainly a long and torturous path. She has already worked hard to create and survive the tension between the good and the bad mother, she has received her golden gowns, met the prince, and wrestled with the father. One is bound to feel that surely this is enough! And in other stories it often is. For example, in the related story from the Brothers Grimm entitled "One Eyes, Two Eyes, Three Eyes," Two Eyes is blessed with a magical tree presenting leaves of silver and fruit of gold – obviously a tree quite like Cinderella's. The tree will surrender its fruit only to Two Eyes, not to her cruel mother and wicked sisters. Then one day a prince approaches. The envious mother and greedy sisters hide Two Eyes under a barrel and attempt to wrest offerings from the tree for the prince. The tree will not yield. Two Eyes then rolls out two golden apples from under the barrel. The prince sees the apples and insists on seeing who is in the barrel. Two Eyes comes out and shows him that the tree gives her its fruit with ease. Then, upon her request, the prince takes her home with him. They fall in love and are married.

Cinderella, although thrice blessed with the golden fruit of the tree, does not simply come out, show herself, and ask to be taken away. A single kiss from the prince cannot awaken this sleeping beauty! Cinderella apparently is still unable to sustain being seen; she returns to her ashes. The ego returns to her complex-ridden state, losing the connection to the Self as well as to the animus. At this point, movement depends upon the arrival of the animus and his engagement with the negative mother archetype at the core of the complexes. As before, change does not evolve from engagement directly between the ego and the negative mother. The animus does arrive, equipped with the slipper as a guide to authenticity. The negative mother complex fights hard to stay in power, offering trimmed-down versions of the shadow, hoping to fool the animus. However, the animus listens carefully to the birds in the tree; he remains open to clues from the spiritual and instinctual realm and does not hesitate to reject falsehood. It is critical at this point to discriminate between the complex-ridden self and the true self. Having seen through falsehood twice, he returns a third time (naturally a third time) and prevails against both the father and the stepmother in summoning Cinderella. Now neither the father complex nor the negative mother complex holds sway; Cinderella's beauty is revealed – the ego is well aligned with the Self and she is free to marry the prince. As they depart, the birds from the tree fly down and sit upon her shoulders. This is a powerful image of wholeness: the bride well supported by spirit and instinct, free to marry the groom. As a final note, the tale emphasizes that the ego, now well related to the rest of the psyche, has a conscious and directed control of rage and envy. Cinderella's guardian birds, perched on her shoulder, peck out the eyes of her stepsisters. Schwartz-Salant suggests that the borderline patient's state is aptly symbolized by the Egyptian eye goddess. This eye "roamed the earth and destroyed everything it saw . . . [with] searing and destructive affects" (Schwartz-Salant 1989, pp. 15–17). It is this "evil eye" of archetypal rage and envy that Cinderella blinds and depotentiates. Thus the power of the shadow is no longer trapped in a complex but is consciously governed by the ego; the archetypal affects are contained and directed.

For some patients, the process of transformation can go relatively smoothly, as it does for Two Eyes. For borderline patients, however, it is typically more convoluted. They, like Cinderella, after having made much progress may well have to return once more to the house of the negative mother. This phase of analysis can be long and very trying. The patient's true self tends to remain tentative and hidden, while her shadow sides attempt to modify themselves so as to remain in power. Typically, the fits of rage become more disguised, the envious attacks more subtle. Within these analytic hours, it is critical but extremely difficult to differentiate justified anger from a well-disguised fit of rage. This is a tough time in the work because the patient is pleased and relieved to have experienced so much change and, like the prince, is at first willing to embrace what looks like the real thing. However, the determined devotion of the patient's animus to look again – to ask, to examine, and to measure – frequently makes this period feel significantly different than the previous times when the patient's ego stood so terribly alone in the face of brutal assaults. Now the animus is present and generally willing to form an energetic alliance with the analyst. Not only the animus but also the acute tuning of spirit and instinct, the birds, work along with the analyst to detect falsehoods. Time after time, trimmed down, complex-laden responses must be rejected. In this manner, extremely intense affects may enter the process without shattering it. The patient is overwhelmed and fragmented less often and the rage and envy become progressively more worked through and integrated. The borderline patient's suffering derives from the state of being fragmented; her healing arrives with increased relatedness, both internally and interpersonally. Slowly but eventually the true self, the true bride, reveals herself and enters the sacred marriage; slowly the patient experiences an increased inner wholeness.

The tale of Cinderella thus poetically portrays the presenting profile of and a path of healing for the female borderline patient. First, Cinderella must wrestle repetitively with an extreme opposition between split poles of the mother archetype. She thus frees herself enough that she is able to meet the animus. However, then she must return to the dynamics of the father complex. Finally, with the support of the animus, she masters the task of discriminating the false bride – her own shadow-driven behavior – from the true bride. She, as ego, is beleaguered throughout this process by attacks from the evil stepmother and stepsisters, that is, by waves of archetypal rage and envy. Her steps through the torturous process of the integration of this rage and envy outline a path of individuation for the borderline patient, the patient smeared with ashes, lost in the darkness.

Schwartz-Salant notes that the suffering of borderline patients is seen in their "anguishing inability to incarnate [the] principle of union," the *coniunctio*. He speculates that the dynamic processes that attend union may reflect the emergence of a new archetypal form in the collective unconscious (ibid., p. 11). The story of Cinderella then could be seen as a story that presents not only a path of healing for the borderline personality but also as a contribution to the emergence of a new archetypal form. This is remarkably similar to conclusions reached by Baring. She suggests that Cinderella personifies aspects of the feminine archetype whose resurrection has been prepared for by those who preserved the mystical traditions and stories that portray "the need to discover the presence of the radiant essence hidden within the myriad forms of life" (Baring 1991, p. 64). She adds that "Cinderella" portrays both the "resurrection" of the feminine archetype and the restoration of the image of union, the sacred marriage, between "nature and spirit, goddess and god [which] has been notably absent in the Judeo-Christian tradition" (ibid., p. 63). It is possible then to conclude that "Cinderella" describes the process which, incarnated in an analysis, enables the borderline patient as an individual, in relationship to her analyst, to wrestle with and ultimately contribute to what are perhaps the most compelling archetypal and cultural dynamics of our times. Indeed, the emergence of this story within an analytic process then may be seen as a personal and individual contribution, through the resurrection of the feminine archetype and the restoration of the image of union, to what Baring refers to as "the new age that is dawning" (ibid.).

## REFERENCES

Abend, S. M., Porter, M. S., and Willick, M. S. 1983. *Borderline Patients: Psychoanalytic Perspectives.* New York: International Universities Press, Inc.

Baring, A. 1991. Cinderella: An interpretation. In *Psyche's Stories: Modern Jungian Interpretaions of Fairy Tales*, vol. 1, M. Stein and L. Corbett, eds. Wilmette, Ill.: Chiron Publications.

Brenman, E. 1988. Cruelty and narrow-mindedness. In *Melanie Klein Today: Developments in Theory and Practice*, vol. 1, E. B. Spillius, ed. London: Routledge.

Cooper, J. C. 1978. *An Illustrated Encyclopedia of Traditional Symbols.* London: Thames & Hudson.

de Vries, A. 1974. *Dictionary of Symbols and Imagery.* Amsterdam: North-Holland Publishing Co.

Herman, J. L. 1992. *Trauma and Recovery.* New York: HarperCollins.

Hunt, M., trans. 1972. *The Complete Grimm's Fairy Tales.* New York: Pantheon Books, Inc.

Jung, C. G. 1971. *Psychological Types. CW*, vol. 6. Princeton, N.J.: Princeton University Press, 1970.

_____. 1967. *Alchemical Studies. CW*, vol. 13. Princeton, N.J.: Princeton University Press, 1983.

Kohut, H. 1984. *How Does Analysis Cure?* London: The University of Chicago Press, Ltd.

Leonard, L. S. 1982. *The Wounded Woman: Healing the Father-Daughter Relationship.* Athens, Ohio: Swallow Press.

Neumann, E. 1952. *Amor and Psyche: The Psychic Development of the Feminine*, R. Manheim, trans. Princeton, N.J.: Princeton University Press.

Schwartz-Salant, N. 1989. *The Borderline Personality: Vision and Healing.* Wilmette, Ill.: Chiron Publications.

Stein, M. 1990. Sibling rivalry and the problem of envy. *Journal of Analytic Psychology* 35:161–174.

Winnicott, D. W. 1971. *Playing and Reality.* New York: Tavistock Publications Ltd./Routledge.

# *Pinocchio*
# A Homoerotic Tale of Male Initiation

## Kenneth W. James

Strictly speaking, the story of Pinocchio is not a fairy tale. It is a novel for children written by Carlo Collodi, the pen name of Carlo Lorenzini. It consists of many tales about the escapades of the puppet without strings; taken as a whole these tales tell of the search for initiation and true autonomy. *Pinocchio* is the story of the initiation of a boy into manhood and the recognition of the homoerotic connection that is required for such an initiation.

The version of *Pinocchio* which is most readily available today is the cartoon version by Walt Disney. This rendition is surprisingly true to the original text, although many of the episodes are absent and others are condensed. A glance at the table of contents of the Collodi book will show how many more episodes are included in the original rendering of the story. In this analysis of the tale, episodes from the original text will be used to exemplify the principles under discussion, but familiarity with the original is not necessary. The phases of development that Pinocchio passes through on his initiatory journey are the same regardless of the version consulted.

## *Pinocchio*

P inocchio is a puppet who becomes a real boy. Carved from a piece of wood and having the capacity to move and speak without the help of a puppeteer, Pinocchio plays tricks on his father/carver Geppetto, who shows concern for the puppet and counsels him on how to behave in the world. Pinocchio chooses to ignore this counsel, showing disobedience in many ways. When a talking cricket reprimands Pinocchio, the puppet takes a hammer and silences him, at least temporarily. Telling Geppetto that he is going to school, Pinocchio instead goes to a puppet show. He is accosted by a fox and a cat, who swindle him out of some gold pieces he had earned at the puppet theater. Pinocchio is hanged on an oak tree and left for dead.

The puppet is saved by a fairy child with blue hair, who has him taken down from the tree. The fairy calls in three doctors, one of whom is the cricket. In the course of his treatment, Pinocchio tells some lies, and his nose grows longer with each untruth. The fairy points this out to him, and Pinocchio feels some shame at being found out. The fairy arranges for his nose to be brought back to its original size, and the puppet goes on his way. Later, he meets with the fairy again, but she is no longer a child and has become a fairy-woman. She promises to help Pinocchio become a real boy the very next day. Pinocchio looks forward to this, but he becomes distracted during a walk to town and goes off on his own once again.

Other misfortunes befall Pinocchio, including being sent to prison. Upon his release, he goes with some other boys to a land of endless entertainment, where he is turned into a donkey. He is thrown into the sea, where he is swallowed by a large fish. Inside the fish he finds Geppetto, who has also been swallowed up. Pinocchio devises a plan for releasing Geppetto and himself from the belly of the fish and carries it out. The puppet then performs other acts of self-sacrifice in his attempts to make reparation to his woodcarver-father. For his efforts, he is transformed by the fairy into a real boy.

## THE INITIATORY MOTIF IN *PINOCCHIO*

The story of Pinocchio is usually thought of as a morality tale showing the consequences of straying from what has been culturally determined to be proper behavior. It has been reduced to a simple fable with a slightly tropological level of meaning and hence dismissed as puerile and insignificant. The figure of Pinocchio is seen as an example of a bad child who becomes good (and therefore "real") through the ministrations of two helpers: the cricket and the fairy. However, if the tale is examined from the perspective of analytical psychology, it becomes apparent that there is more to the story of the wooden boy than a simple morality tale.

*Pinocchio* is a story of masculine initiation that occurs via a homoerotic connection. Men initiate men and women initiate women; hence to become a "real boy," a truly autonomous male, Pinocchio must be initiated through his connection with another male. As so often happens in life, initiation is confused in this tale with mere separateness and Pinocchio starts his life believing, because he has no strings, that he already is a fully initiated, and hence "real," male. He discovers this is false by the end of the book, but throughout the text his escapades indicate that unconsciously he realizes that, although "autonomous" in the sense of being separate, he must achieve his initiation through his interactions with other male figures. Unfortunately he experiences many failures, since instead of an erotic connection with a male he experiences shadow links with them.

The term "homoerotic" will require explanation. It refers to the erotic connection that may obtain between two individuals of the same gender. This eros connection is based on a psychic relationship between the individuals, a connection that goes beyond the more common logos-based connection that is experienced in human interaction. Homoeros may be concretized in homosexual relationship, but this is only a particular channeling of the homoerotic impulse. Eros-based connections to others have an initiatory capacity, since they can open each participant to a new level of being; sexual congress does not necessarily do this. In order to progress from a state of dependency and uninitiatedness to the state of the initiated autonomous male, an eros-based connection to an initiated male figure is required. The specific structure and dynamics of this connection may involve an external male or an inner male figure. It is this search, which seems to be an instinctive part of the psyche of boys, that is scrutinized in the story of Pinocchio.

As so often happens, the push from within for a connection to a significant same-gender figure as initiator is sidetracked in Pinocchio by attachments to various figures of evil or shadow. Unable to access his own power and authority, he becomes attracted by the projection of this power and authority onto others, who are inevitably shadowy or evil. Pinocchio also makes the mistake made by so many immature, uninitiated members of society: he assumes that he is already fully autonomous and initiated, and he manifests this mistaken assumption through the lie. The lie may be seen as an immature manifestation of autonomy, a sort of negative separation ritual placing a naive boundary between the liar and authority figures, partners, and consensus reality as a whole. Neither of these activities (projection and connection with the shadow, or lying), foster initiation; crossing the threshold to a truly new level of being (i.e., becoming initiated) requires the presence of eros, a positive connection on a psychic level. It is this that Pinocchio eventually experiences, although not until it is over does he realize the fruits of his initiatory experience.

In a way, Pinocchio's lie is the first action he performs that lays claim, albeit prematurely, to true autonomy. Through the lie, the initiatory process is begun and the homoerotic drive is activated. Although a phrase such as "seeking a positive male role model" may be easier to accept, it does not express the absolutely pivotal role such a connection plays in the psychic life of the developing male. Calling this a homoerotic drive emphasizes its critical value in the economy of the psyche.

The five steps of Pinocchio's initiation may serve as a skeletal structure for the initiatory journey facing all males in modern Western society. The first step in Pinocchio's initiation is his creation at the hands of his father Geppetto. The second step is the separation, which in *Pinocchio* is exemplified by physical acts of separation and by lies. Next comes a period of exploration, during which Pinocchio meets two friends who are very critical from the perspective of analytical psychology: the cricket and the fairy. The fourth stage in his initiatory journey is the dissolution, which is the stage in which Pinocchio submits to the sacrifice. Finally, the fifth stage of transformation occurs, in which Pinocchio actualizes that which he claimed prematurely in the second stage: his realness, his true autonomy as an initiated member of society. Each of these stages will be examined through an analysis of events in *Pinocchio*, in order to more fully develop the initiatory theme present in this children's story.

The particular trappings of the story – and the fact that at the story's end, when Pinocchio becomes real, he is permitted to live out his life as "a well-behaved boy" – do not mitigate the initiatory nature of the tale. The story is designed to be told to children, probably by their parents, and nothing would be so threatening to an adult as to read to their children a manual outlining a method for becoming fully functioning adults. So in order for the truth in the tale to be passed on, it must be cloaked in narrative "accidents" that hide the story's true significance. Thus it ever is with fairy tales, other forms of art, and dreams.

## STAGE ONE: PINOCCHIO'S CREATION

Pinocchio is made of wood, and in the popular renditions of the story the source of the wood is not discussed. In Collodi's version, however, the wood from which Pinocchio is carved is very special indeed. And as if to emphasize subtly that the story of this boy will be the story of all males, not one but two men are involved in the discovery of the wood and in shaping its ultimate destiny.

The wood that will become Pinocchio is found on the doorstep of a carpenter named Master Antonio, known more familiarly as Master Cherry. Master Cherry comes upon the piece of wood and is about to shape it into a table leg when it speaks to him. He is stunned and falls to the ground. He is found there by his friend Master Geppetto, who desired to get some wood from the carpenter so that he might make a puppet. Master Cherry presents Geppetto with the talking wood, which then hits Geppetto on his shins. Geppetto, believing Master Cherry to be the one who hit him, begins to fight with the carpenter. Both the men are wounded, but Geppetto gets to take the wood off to his own house.

Hence Pinocchio is born, so to speak, from two men. Their connection is physical, although instead of love-making they engage in fisticuffs. Nevertheless, Pinocchio's start is through the interaction of his two male parents; this suggests that the story about to be told is a story about men interacting with men and the forms that interaction may take.

Almost instantly, Pinocchio begins to play tricks on the old man Geppetto. In spite of this, the wood carver's first act toward Pinocchio, after the sculpting is finished, is to teach the puppet to walk. Walking, which requires standing up on one's own feet, is an early motor act that betokens autonomy and fosters physical separation leading to exploration. It is Geppetto who teaches Pinocchio this skill, an act that adumbrates Pinocchio's later initiation. In fact, Geppetto not only teaches Pinocchio to walk but, later in the story, when Pinocchio's feet are burned off, carves new ones for him. Thus the link between Geppetto and Pinocchio is that of initiator to initiate; but much must be endured by both before the act of initiation will be complete.

In an interesting vignette, when Pinocchio first discovers that his feet have burned off, the puppet cries out that "I shall have to walk on my knees for the rest of my life." Being brought to one's knees in submission is almost the psychic polar opposite of being an initiated individual, so Geppetto's actions in making new feet for Pinocchio may also be interpreted as an attempt to save the puppet from submission, from an uninitiated journey through life.

## STAGE TWO: THE SEPARATION

Pinocchio separates from Geppetto in several ways. First, he tries to escape by running away. Geppetto, chasing him, becomes progressively angrier, and bystanders feel that he will end up abusing the puppet so they give Pinocchio his freedom and send Geppetto to prison. In this first attempt at autonomy Pinocchio meets the cricket, who psychologically may be seen as the voice of the conscience, one aspect of the superego. The other aspect, the ego ideal, is absent from this meeting, which further suggests that the entire story is a search for that ego ideal or that exemplar toward which initiation leads. Pinocchio ends up crushing the cricket for telling the truth: that Pinocchio is a puppet with a wooden head. The cricket's statement translates psychologically into the fact that Pinocchio is not truly autonomous and is not yet initiated. Pinocchio cannot bear to hear this, and so he crushes the cricket with a hammer.

In his prematurely separate state, Pinocchio is unable to nourish himself; an attempt to make an omelet results in simply the freeing of a little chick from its shell. When Pinocchio ends up with his feet burned, Geppetto, now freed from prison, finds him and carves some new feet for him. Pinocchio then exhibits the next move in his drive for separation: he lies. His lie is not so much a direct misrepresentation as it is a promise that he cannot fulfill. He promises to be good in the future once he receives new feet. Geppetto, with the wisdom perhaps gathered from his own boyhood experiences, tells Pinocchio that lying is a common device used by boys to get what they want. Pinocchio counters by protesting that he is better than all other boys and he always speaks the truth. Such inflation, which often accompanies lying, serves to reinforce the effort that Pinocchio is exerting in his drive to be separate from Geppetto.

It is significant that the lies Pinocchio tells at this point in the story are lies about the future: he promises to do things that he has no intention of doing or that he is unable to do. At a later stage in his development, Pinocchio will again lie, only these lies will be a more deliberate misrepresentation of historical fact and will be told to the beautiful female fairy with blue hair, an anima figure. This second attempt to assert his absolute (and absolutely mistaken) separateness will also fail.

STAGE THREE: EXPLORATION

Pinocchio's explorations are marked by encounters with shadow figures that hold an attraction for him. He inappropriately attempts to act out his drive for initiation with these figures, each time falling more deeply into a state of almost total loss of identity. Thus it can be seen that these explorations are in the service of initiation, although they seem to be wrong turns at the time. There are many of them, and they all involve Pinocchio in interaction with other male figures. This most protracted of all the stages on the initiatory journey is also marked by the appearance of a contrasexual figure, an anima-companion. The sole female figure in the story appears as the fairy with the blue hair ("the Blue Fairy" in the Disney version). It is Pinocchio's relationship with her that leads him to make the sacrifice that will result in his initiation. Male initiation, although based on the energies of the homoerotic, must include the guidance and cooperation of the feminine as well; a fully initiated male is capable of significant relationships with both men and women.

In order to get money to see a puppet show, Pinocchio sells the spelling book that Geppetto bought for him. At the puppet show, Pinocchio meets Master Fire-Eater, who threatens to burn the puppet. When Pinocchio gets him to relent, Master Fire-Eater then threatens to burn another puppet, but Pinocchio successfully pleads for mercy. The next day, Master Fire-Eater gives Pinocchio five gold pieces to be given to Geppetto and sends him home.

Master Fire-Eater may be seen as a negative father figure, a figure of darkness, who sends Pinocchio back to his positive father via the gift of gold for Geppetto. If the tension between these polarities can be successfully held, the positive and negative father figures can serve as the initiators of the puppet-boy. The puppet is unable to hold the tension, however, and Pinocchio gets waylaid once again.

This time, it is the figures of Cat and Fox who trick Pinocchio out of some of his money. Feeling that Cat and Fox can help him make even more money, Pinocchio goes with them and winds up paying for their lodging and food and ultimately being abandoned by them, only to be accosted by some assassins on the road. He takes a beating at the hands of the assassins and ends up appealing for help at the home of the fairy with the blue hair. She does not help him at this point, and he is ultimately captured by the assassins and hanged on the branch of an oak tree. As he hangs there, he cries out for his father.

The promise of more gold symbolizes the potential for empowerment in worldly terms, but this empowerment is not true initiation. It is merely an accretion of material deemed by the world to be valuable. The mere possession of something outside of oneself is not the same as true initiation, and Pinocchio ends up hanging on the tree crying out a wish that Geppetto were there with him. He cries, it seems, for a true initiator. But he is saved, at least this time, by the fairy. As Pinocchio explores the world, he accepts the aid of this anima figure who supports him and heals his wounds.

Seeing Pinocchio on the oak, the fairy has him brought into her home and sends for three doctors—one of whom, the talking cricket, once again tells the truth about Pinocchio's uninitiated state. While he is not as violent toward the cricket as he was earlier, Pinocchio simply closes his eyes and does not listen to him. The fairy then takes on the responsibility of giving Pinocchio the medicine the doctors have prescribed. In a conversation with her, Pinocchio lies and his nose grows; the fairy immediately recognizes his lie and tells him so. This causes Pinocchio much discomfort, and the fairy takes pity on him. After fixing his nose, she offers to take Pinocchio in and to bring Geppetto to her home as well. Pinocchio asks instead if he may go to meet Geppetto, and the fairy consents. She probably knows that Pinocchio will not succeed so easily but will have even more explorations, so she tells him simply, "Be careful not to lose yourself."

As an anima figure, the fairy helps Pinocchio recollect all that he has been through and to examine it, at least on a preliminary level. His stay with her is a major point of recollection during the exploration stage of his development. The existence of the stage of exploration seems to be constitutive to the path of initiation, but unless the exploratory experiences are re-collected they do not foster change or growth. Exploration is only truly so when the explorer is changed by the experience; merely going from thrill to thrill does not constitute exploration. The fairy serves as a means of recollection for Pinocchio, to save him from becoming lost in this exploratory stage and not progressing along his path toward initiation.

Other escapades follow during Pinocchio's stage of exploration. He meets up again with Cat and Fox and loses the rest of his money to them. He is jailed, gains his release, is captured by a farmer and proves to be worthy of his freedom, and comes again upon the fairy. She has grown since last Pinocchio saw her, becoming a woman-fairy. She tells him that she is now old enough to be his mother. Pinocchio is intrigued by her growth and asks if he will be able to grow. The fairy tells him that only real boys are capable of growth, not puppets. Pinocchio then discovers what he must do to become a real boy; he learns from the fairy what must be done to complete his initiation.

In a sense, the fairy becomes Pinocchio's ego ideal, since she has grown and offers him a glimpse of what growth would mean. But she also serves as a reminder to him of what is really important: the inner person. It was because of Pinocchio's good heart, which the fairy recognized, that he is being offered this instruction on how to become real. It is as though she tells him that the particular acts he has performed on his exploratory journey are not as important as the inner stance he has held regarding the more significant events of his psychic life.

STAGE FOUR: DISSOLUTION

Following the advice of the fairy, Pinocchio begins to attend school but soon is involved in fights with the other boys and runs away to escape punishment. He is found and forgiven by the fairy, who promises to make him a real boy the following day. But Pinocchio instead leaves the fairy and travels to Boobyland, otherwise known as the Land of Cocagne, where he becomes a donkey instead of a boy.

This stage marks the nadir of Pinocchio's descent. He betrays the fairy, perhaps knowing that an initiation at her hands would not be a true initiation. (She probably knew this as well.) He goes instead to a place where he loses his identity as a puppet and becomes something that, though real, is much less desirable than being a boy. It is at this point, when all seems lost, that events take a turn that brings Pinocchio to the threshold of initiation and transformation.

Desirous of Pinocchio's donkey skin to make a drumhead, a man throws him into the water to drown. Thrust deeply into the unconscious, from which he was acting blindly for so long, Pinocchio is saved by the fairy/anima, who sends fish to transform him back into a puppet. Pinocchio swims away and is swallowed by a gigantic dog-fish. In the belly of this fish he finds Geppetto, who was also swallowed by the monster. Having no concern for his own safety, Pinocchio leads Geppetto out of the dogfish, but the old man becomes ill. After swimming for a long time, Pinocchio becomes so fatigued that he is on the verge of drowning, but he manages to come to shore with Geppetto. In a series of events dictated not by his own self-interest but concern for the well-being of Geppetto, Pinocchio repudiates the Cat and Fox, asks for forgiveness from the cricket, and performs hard labor merely to earn a cup of milk for the old man. He also engages in basket making, which brings in more money to pay for daily living expenses, and makes a wheelchair for his father, Geppetto. Finally, he gives all the money he has to help the fairy out of a predicament; he allows his libido to flow freely toward both the masculine and feminine aspects of life.

During the stage of dissolution, Pinocchio experiences an emptying of all that he has clung to as his own; even his identity as a puppet is called into question. Little by little, Pinocchio willingly relinquishes all that has been his in favor of the welfare of Geppetto. He sacrifices himself to empower this man whom he loves; Geppetto in his weakness becomes the agent of Pinocchio's initiation. Therein lies the secret of the initiate. One cannot sacrifice what one does not possess, and to sacrifice oneself is to be self-possessed; such a connection with one's essence is the hallmark of the initiated person or, in Pinocchio's case, the initiated male. Through his actions on Geppetto's behalf, Pinocchio opens himself to the next stage in his initiatory journey.

## STAGE FIVE: TRANSFORMATION

Following this period of dissolution, or emptying of all that was familiar and dear to him, Pinocchio falls asleep and has a dream.

In the dream the fairy comes to him, speaks to him, and tells him that all the sins he has committed, all the lies he has told, all the egocentric actions he has taken to save himself from the truth of his uninitiated state – all this will be forgiven. He awakens to find himself a real boy instead of a puppet. He is truly autonomous, and like all real individuals, is now capable of growth. It is at this point that the attraction to the anima-figure can be actualized, or played out in lived time. It was the fairy who introduced to Pinocchio the possibility of growth, and now that the realness of his own gender has been affirmed, future growth lies in coming to an understanding of the other, in all its manifestations. Clearly, growth is needed since Pinocchio is but a boy; there is work to be done. Because it was the anima that first presented the prospect of development to the then-wooden boy, it is to the anima that the newly-initiated one will most likely turn in an attempt to find out what comes next.

With this realization, the story of Pinocchio ends. It is a story of initiation, specifically of the homoerotic drive toward initiation that is active in males. Initiation is not an ending but permits a new beginning that will allow for connection and generativity that would be impossible for an uninitiated person. Other stories will tell those tales; what Pinocchio expresses is the change from being merely separate to being real, capable of growth and self-direction.

# About the Authors

*Volume 3*

**Murray Stein**, Ph.D., is the author of *Solar Conscience/Lunar Conscience* (Chiron), *In MidLife* (Spring), and *Jung's Treatment of Christianity* (Chiron), and of many papers in Jungian psychology. He is editor of *Jungian Analysis* (Open Court), *Jung's Challenge to Contemporary Religion* (Chiron), and numerous other collections. He has a private practice in Wilmette, Illinois, and teaches at the C. G. Jung Institute of Chicago.

**Lionel Corbett** is a Jungian analyst in private practice in Santa Fe, New Mexico.

**Daniel A. Lindley, Jr.**, is an associate professor of English at the University of Illinois, a psychotherapist in private practice, and a candidate at the C. G. Jung Institute of Chicago. He is the author of *This Rough Magic: The Life of Teaching* (forthcoming from Greenwood Press) and numerous articles on teaching.

**Nancy Dougherty**, A.C.S.W., is a Jungian analyst in private practice in Birmingham, Michigan. She is a member of the Chicago Society of Jungian Analysts.

**Joel Ryce-Menuhin** is a training analyst with the Independent Group of Analytical Psychologists, London, and founder of the British and Irish Branch of the International Society for Sandplay Therapy. He is the author of *The Self in Early Childhood* (Columbia University Press) and *Jungian Sandplay: The Wonderful Therapy* (Routledge), and editor of *Jung and the Monotheisms* (forthcoming from Routledge).

**Jacqueline J. West**, Ph.D., received her analytical training at the Rocky Mountain Region of the Inter-Regional Society of Jungian Analysts. She has a private practice in Santa Fe, New Mexico, and is particularly interested in borderline phenomenology, the nature of archetypal affect, and the analysis of art and culture.

**Kenneth W. James** is a Jungian analyst in private practice in Evanston, Illinois, and a faculty member at Northeastern Illinois University, where he is the director of the Learning Disabilities Clinic. His professional interests include analytic perspectives on medieval apocalyptic imagery, number symbolism in dreams, myth, and scripture, and archetypal imagery.

CPSIA information can be obtained
at www.ICGtesting.com
Printed in the USA
FFOW01n2015010714
6139FF